The
CREDIT CARD
INDUSTRY
A History

TWAYNE'S EVOLUTION OF AMERICAN BUSINESS SERIES

INDUSTRIES, INSTITUTIONS, AND ENTREPRENEURS

Edwin J. Perkins
SERIES EDITOR
UNIVERSITY OF SOUTHERN CALIFORNIA

The
CREDIT CARD
INDUSTRY
A History

LEWIS MANDELL

TWAYNE PUBLISHERS □ BOSTON
A Division of G. K. Hall & Co.

The Credit Card Industry: A History
Lewis Mandell

Twayne's Evolution of American Business Series
Industries, Institutions, and Entrepreneurs
No. 4.

Copyright 1990 by G. K. Hall & Co.
All rights reserved.
Published by Twayne Publishers
A division of G. K. Hall & Co.
70 Lincoln Street
Boston, Massachusetts 02111

Copyediting supervised by Barbara Sutton.
Book production and design by Gabrielle B. MᶜDonald.
Typeset in Aldus with Optima display type
by Huron Valley Graphics, Inc. of Ann Arbor, Michigan.

The paper used in this publication meets the minimum requirements
of American National Standard for Information Sciences—Permanence
of Paper for Printed Library Materials, ANSI Z39.48-1984.⊗™

Printed and bound in the United States of America.

Library of Congress Cataloging-in-Publication Data

Mandell, Lewis.
    The credit card industry : a history / Lewis Mandell.
        p.   cm. — (Twayne's evolution of American business series ;
    no. 4)
        Includes bibliographical references.
        1. Credit cards—United States—History.   2. Consumer credit—
    United States—History.   I. Title.   II. Series.
    HG3756.U54M25   1990
    332.7'65'0973—dc20   90-4406
                                                                    CIP

0-8057-9810-2 (alk. paper). 10 9 8 7 6 5 4 3 2 1
0-8057-9816-1 (pbk. alk. paper). 10 9 8 7 6 5 4 3 2 1
First published 1990.

CONTENTS

PREFACE

IN THE SPRING OF 1979, I WAS SITTING IN MY apartment in Tel Aviv when the telephone rang. It was Spencer Nilson calling from California. The writer and publisher of the *Nilson Report* on the credit card industry had tracked me down to the Middle East, where I was a visiting professor at Tel Aviv University, to ask me to write a history of credit cards.

At first I demurred, but Spencer persisted, telling me that innovations in the manufacture, marketing, and uses of the modern credit card were well detailed in his bimonthly newsletter that he had been writing for decades, but that there was a larger story to be told. The facts needed to be placed into a historical context to permit broader analysis of the growth of the spending-and-lending phenomenon. My job would be to pull the available information together, add material on the history of credit cards prior to the first publication of Spencer's newsletter, bring my analytical insights to bear, and create a chronological narrative history of the industry, peopled with its lead players.

Finally, I agreed to write a relatively short, readable, and comprehensive chronicle of the credit card that would be accessible to the lay reader. With this objective in mind, and making extensive use of the *Nilson Report* for source material, I forsook the use of source citations. Identification of sources of statistics and news items by individual footnotes has been subordinated to the goal of presenting the reader with a smooth-flowing summary of crucial developments in the industry. Since the book was originally intended to be a joint effort based on the newsletter, some phrases and even whole sentences appear in the words of Spencer Nilson.

I did not publish at that time what I had written, because Spencer determined that it was still too academic for his readership of industry professionals. He urged me to seek publication on my own, which I did, but I soon turned my attention to other projects and for a few years put this one out of my thoughts. Then Fred Carstensen, a colleague at the University of

Connecticut who teaches economic history, told me about a new series in business history launched by Twayne Publishers. I sent my manuscript to the series editor, Edwin Perkins of the University of Southern California, who encouraged me to bring it up to date and polish it for publication. At Twayne, senior editor Meghan Wander found a free-lance editor, Michael Casey, who was willing to work with me to restructure and recast the book to appeal to a wider readership. Michael Casey's interest and enthusiasm, as well as his editorial talents, have contributed a great deal to this book.

In making acknowledgments, my greatest debt is to Spencer Nilson, not only for proposing the project and supplying much of the source material for it, but also for introducing me to some of the pioneers of the credit card industry. One such pioneer, Al Bloomingdale, granted me a very long interview, which forms the basis of Chapter 1 on the founding of Diners Club. This interview was given shortly before his death and contains a great deal of previously unreported information. I am also indebted to a graduate assistant, Lucia Fetherstone, who helped with the library research, and to my wife, Nancy, whose long-term encouragement helped this project to closure.

Lewis Mandell

University of Connecticut

INTRODUCTION

"I'll charge it."

THIS PHRASE IS THE SLOGAN FOR A GENERA-
tion of consumers who have grown up in the post–World War II era.
Virtually unknown at the beginning of the century, by 1988 there were
nearly 1.25 billion credit cards in circulation worldwide. In the United
States alone, according to the *Nilson Report* (see reference in Bibliography),
consumers charged nearly $375 billion on their credit cards—12.6 percent
of total consumer spending for all goods and services. Armed with billions
of credit cards, shoppers, businesspeople, and travelers of all economic and
social backgrounds from around the world now charge everything from
vacations and business trips to groceries and hair dryers. Whether we call
them bank cards, gas cards, retail cards, travel and entertainment cards, or
simply the more familiar "plastic," there is little doubt that the credit card
has revolutionized the marketplace. These thin, wallet-sized, plastic rectangles with their unobtrusively sophisticated magnetic stripes are the keys
that unlock the electronic vaults of banks, automated teller machines
(ATMs), and cash dispensers around the world. They have become an essen-
tial element of daily life. With a credit card, you can buy yourself a new car.
Without it, you cannot even rent one.

The concept of credit has existed and been in use almost as long as
there has been civilization. It predates, by a considerable length of time,
the use of money, and written references to it appear as far back as in the
Code of Hammurabi, established around 1750 B.C. What is very different
about credit in the twentieth century is the way and the extent to which it
is used. From its beginnings in antiquity, however, credit has been used as
a selling tool, to bind customers to a particular vendor, and to allow them
to acquire more substantial goods for which they do not have the necessary capital.

The modern concept of credit dates back to the late eighteenth and early nineteenth centuries when liberal British economists, arguing against economic restrictions on credit, helped to overcome the centuries-long condemnation of consumer credit. While Europeans would continue to argue over the dangers and merits of consumer credit, the citizens of the young United States readily embraced the radical new idea. They recognized the need for a flexible system of credit in a large country with a far-flung populace and a voracious appetite for capital.

Consumer credit in the United States, particularly in the form of installment and revolving credit plans, grew quickly during the years of post–Civil War industrialization. As families dispersed across the expanding country, they were forced to rely upon formal credit provided by merchants and financial intermediaries. After the First World War, the widespread sale of automobiles, washing machines, vacuum cleaners, and other big-ticket household durables increased the need for credit and the consequent use of credit cards. The expansion of consumer credit was slowed by the Great Depression and then halted by wartime restrictions in the 1940s. But the return to prosperity following the war set the stage for credit vehicles that would be widely accepted and easy to use.

The forerunners of universal credit cards were the storespecific cards issued by a small number of U.S. hotels, oil companies, and department stores in the early twentieth century. Retail cards had two purposes: to identify a customer with a charge account, and to provide merchants with a mechanism for keeping a record of customer purchases.

For retailers, credit cards were merely a logical extension of already existing installment plans. In 1914, several retailers began to issue cards to their wealthier customers to bind them to the store as well as to generate sales of higher priced items. In 1928, retailers began to issue "charga-plates," which were really embossed-metal address plates. Over the next thirty years, various innovations such as minimum monthly payments, finance charges, and the thirty-day grace period were developed and adopted by the large retailers to maximize profits from their credit operations.

Following on the heels of the retail cards, gasoline cards, which grew with the proliferation of the automobile, and, later, airline cards added to the growing number of credit card operations. In the early 1920s, oil companies began to issue "courtesy" cards with which travelers could charge purchases to their accounts at any of an oil company's affiliates. These cards did not have a revolving credit feature and were costly for the issuers. However, because of competitive pressures within the industry, oil companies were willing to absorb the losses to maintain market share. Credit cards were one of the few ways in which an oil company could differentiate itself from its competitors. In 1936, the growing airline industry, led by American Airlines, formed its own credit system called the Universal Air Travel Plan (UATP). Initially a coupon book that was issued against a deposit,

UATP's credit plan would later evolve into a credit card operation quite similar to and in direct competition with the universal third-party cards.

The era of the modern, third-party universal card began with the formation of Diners Club in 1949. In the spring of that year, Alfred Bloomingdale, Frank McNamara, and Ralph Snyder conceived a plan for a new type of credit card. Unlike the retail and gas credit cards, which were restricted in use to those industries, theirs would be a "universal" card that allowed its holder to purchase goods and services at a variety of establishments across the country. A notable aspect of their plan was the introduction of a third party into the credit equation. Their company would become the middleman between the consumer and the merchant, extending credit to one, providing customers for the other, and charging both for their services. With no goods to sell or customer loyalty to promote, their interest was purely financial. They conceived of credit as a product to be sold, an end in itself rather than simply a means to an end, and the primary vehicle for extending credit was the credit card. There was no precedent for a company such as the one they envisaged. However, like all good entrepreneurs, they trusted their instincts and forged ahead.

With only $75,000 in the bank but confident of the viability of their idea, they made the decision to launch their new company. The revenues needed to finance the company were generated by a merchant discount, initially 7 percent of the purchase, and by a monthly fee for cardholders. (Interest charges on unpaid balances were a later innovation of the bank card companies.)

Expansion involved marketing to two parties, the merchants and the customers. But Diners Club faced a true chicken-or-egg situation: consumers would not sign up for the card unless it was accepted by a large number of merchants, and merchants would not sign up until they saw a demand for the card from their customers.

Merchants also balked at the discount demanded by the credit card company. Another obstacle facing the new universal credit card was the resistance of industries such as the airlines, oil companies, and the larger retailers who already issued their own credit cards. In addition to their reluctance to pay a discount to a third party, merchants feared that the acceptance of a third-party card would weaken their relationship with their customers.

Despite these early difficulties, the founders of Diners Club remained convinced that a market existed for universal credit cards. Postwar America was ripe for the burgeoning credit industry. For the first time in the country's history, the majority of Americans were earning income in excess of what it took to pay for their basic needs. In addition, the necessities of war had produced a massive U.S. industrial base, which was prepared to produce consumer durables at a tremendous pace: stoves, refrigerators, automobiles—the more goods consumers purchased, the more goods industry produced, in ever increasing variety and number.

Diners Club's perseverance allowed it to expand its operations across the United States. The primary user of the new universal card was the salesman who could charge meals at restaurants while entertaining clients or while on the road. This market accounted for its name, "Diners Club," and for the general classification of the various companies that soon emulated its operation as travel and entertainment (T&E) card companies.

In 1958, American Express, the traveler's check giant, and Carte Blanche, the private credit card operation of the Hilton Hotel Corporation, both entered the universal credit card field. The same year, the country's largest and second-largest banks, Bank of America and Chase Manhattan Bank, also launched credit card operations. They were soon joined by a number of smaller concerns all looking to test the waters in this promising but still uncertain industry.

The next few years saw a gradual shakeout of the industry as companies struggled to learn and overcome the idiosyncracies of the credit card business. Some, such as Chase Manhattan, which sold its operation in 1962, were unable to make their companies a viable concern. Many of the operational problems they faced, such as processing difficulties and various forms of credit card fraud, would continue to plague the industry for the next twenty years. The primary obstacle to growth, however, was the lack of a national network, which particularly affected the many smaller banks that maintained local credit card operations.

In 1966, Bank of America took a major step toward solving this problem by deciding to license its new BankAmericard across the United States. The decision by the nation's largest bank to expand its operations across the country prompted several other large banks to join together to form a second national card system, known as the Interbank Card Association. The companies now needed to establish a similarly large cardholder base to support these new large-scale operations. With national networks in place, the stage was set for a major marketing war for new customers.

In the late 1960s, both Bank of America and Interbank launched a series of carefully calculated mass mailings of unsolicited credit cards, initiating a period of tremendous growth in the credit card industry. Through these marketing blitzes, both companies succeeded in signing up millions of cardholders in a very short time. Lured by the prospect of a much larger cardholder base, merchants rushed to join the two national credit systems. This, in turn, prompted a number of banks that were still operating independent credit card plans to join one of the credit systems. By 1978, more than 11,000 banks had joined one or both of these networks. Annual sales had topped $44 billion, and fifty-two million Americans had at least two bank credit cards.

During this expansion phase, the companies not unexpectedly suffered through numerous growing pains. Before the industry had jelled into recognizable form in the late 1960s, separate legislation was not deemed necessary for credit cards. As the credit card wove its way into the fabric of everyday life, however, it came under increasing scrutiny from the government, inevitably leading to increased regulation. Ironically, the event that triggered the movement toward regulation was the same mass mailing of unsolicited credit cards that had also led to the industry's rapid growth.

While the companies had expected to incur losses due to fraud in the wake of the mass mailings, they had not been prepared for the many legal questions that arose. What was to be done to protect the many innocent customers who were billed and hounded for charges made on cards they had never ordered or received? If a card was lost or stolen, how was the liability of the cardholder, versus that of the issuer, to be determined? What guidelines were to be followed in settling billing errors caused by the overloading of limited computer systems, and who was to set those guidelines? With consumer credit becoming a virtual necessity, how were consumers to be assured of equal access? And what was to be done about providing or limiting access to the credit histories being amassed by credit companies on millions of cardholders?

The government enacted a number of bills to address these problems, beginning with the Federal Trade Commission's 1970 banning of mailings of unsolicited credit cards. The Fair Credit Billing Act, passed in 1972, designated the Federal Reserve Board as the first formal regulatory body for the industry, with complete jurisdiction over billing practices. The Federal Privacy Act, enacted the following year, provided protection for credit customers from unauthorized use of their credit records. And in 1977, the Equal Credit Opportunity Act became law, prohibiting the use of race, sex, creed, national origin, or marital status as criteria for issuing or denying credit.

Growth also brought consolidation as the industry came to be dominated by an increasingly smaller number of banks and credit card companies. Capitalizing upon their superior marketing ability, larger banks such as Citibank and Continental Bank of Chicago steadily increased their market share at the expense of smaller banks. Another major factor contributing to the consolidation of the industry was the lack of identification by most cardholders with the bank that issued their credit card. As far as most cardholders were concerned, they owned a Visa or Master Charge card, not a Chase Manhattan or First National card. (BankAmericard had changed its name to Visa in 1976 to develop a more international image. Master Charge would do the same in 1980, changing its name to MasterCard.) In retrospect, this concentration of power appears to have been an inevitable development in an industry so dependent on economies of scale and worldwide operational capabilities. By the end of the 1970s, fifty banks issued over half of all bank credit cards in the United States.

Although some banks continued with their own private-label cards, the vast majority issued either Master Charge or Visa. In 1970, Master Charge had enjoyed a solid lead over BankAmericard in both the domestic and international markets. But as the decade neared its end, Visa's innovative and aggressive marketing, and the able and steady leadership of Visa president Dee Hock, enabled it to overtake and eventually pass its rival. From 1969 to 1981, the number of participating MasterCard banks increased from 4,461 to 12,504, while the number of participating Visa banks increased from 3,751 to 12,518. By the late 1980s, Visa had increased its lead over its rival to more than a third.

The competition between the two came to a head in the mid-1970s over the issue of duality. Duality referred to the issuance of both major credit cards by the same bank. Initially, both Visa and MasterCard had prohibited this practice. However, under pressure from the courts, which maintained that such a prohibition violated antitrust laws, they were forced to give the banks free rein to issue both cards. The onset of duality initiated a tremendous marketing war as banks fought over the dual charge card business of merchants. Banks also stepped up their marketing efforts to consumers in an attempt to place a second card in the hands of all their cardholders. The results of this marketing war for the banks were lower revenues and increased costs.

Competition and growth also led to increased concentration in the T&E card industry. With its far superior resources, American Express quickly overtook both Diners Club and Carte Blanche. By 1970, it had twice the number of cardholders as Diners Club, and four times the number of Carte Blanche cardholders. By 1976, it had pulled ahead even further: its cardholder base numbered nearly seven and a half times that of Diners Club, and ten times that of Carte Blanche.

The proliferation of all types of credit cards added to American Express's advantage. Cardholders saw little reason to hold more than one T&E card, and American Express became that card. Eventually both Diners Club and Carte Blanche were purchased by Citibank, which was much better able to compete with American Express. But even Citibank was never able to threaten seriously American Express's firm hold on the first spot in the industry. Today, American Express has more than twelve times as many cardholders as the other two combined.

Domestic expansion of the credit card industry was paralleled by similar growth in the international markets. Credit cards had existed in Europe since the early 1950s, when the British Hotel and Restaurant Association had begun issuing the BHR credit card. American credit card companies had also entered the market early in that decade because they quickly realized that theirs was a readily exportable financial service. Diners Club had moved abroad through franchises soon after its inception. It maintained its leadership in Europe long after American Express had overtaken its U.S. operations, although American Express's superior resources eventually allowed it to gain a dominating position in the international markets as well.

The bank cards had a slower start expanding overseas. In 1972, BankAmericard claimed to operate in seventy-one countries worldwide, but except for Great Britain, where it had purchased the Barclay's card, its coverage was poor at best. Many European banks balked at signing an agreement with BankAmericard because of their fear of aligning themselves with Bank of America, the world's largest bank. This fear worked to Interbank's advantage, enabling it to negotiate an interchange agreement with EuroCard, the largest universal card system in Europe, and Access, the largest card system in Great Britain. The small number of U.S. retailers, that had operations in Europe, such as Sears, also introduced their own proprietary cards with much success.

Visa and MasterCard were less successful in Japan. The JCB bank, an American Express affiliate, led the market by a comfortable margin, with nearly twice the combined cardholders of Visa and MasterCard, and nearly twice those of its closest Japanese competitor. Although it started out behind many other countries in the size of its credit market, Japan quickly caught up. By 1980, it had passed all the European nations and ranked second behind only the United States in the number of credit cards issued.

Even as the credit card companies pushed to expand their markets abroad, they continued their assault at home on those domestic industries that had initially rejected them: the oil companies, the airlines, and most importantly, the large national retailers. Both the bank cards and the T&E cards had enjoyed access to the gas and airline industries since the 1960s. However, they had never achieved the domination of those industries that they desired. Although the bank cards were able to gain access to the gasoline market, events such as the Arab oil embargo in 1973 and the oil crisis of 1979 limited their success by allowing the oil companies to occasionally bar them from gas companies across the country. Similarly, while the bank cards had enjoyed access to the airline industry for many years, they faced stiff competition when the airlines launched their own T&E cards in the mid-1970s.

As important as the gasoline and airline industries were to the credit card companies, the real prize was the retail industry. The large retail stores, which had operated credit card plans for much of the twentieth century, issued far more cards than all of the third-party companies combined and continued to do so into the 1980s. In 1981, Sears alone issued more cards than either Visa or MasterCard.

Unlike third-party issuers, who run their credit operations to make a profit, retailers saw their credit card operations as a means to facilitate sales and ensure customer loyalty. Generally, retail credit card operations broke even or operated at a small loss. The larger retailers, such as Sears, Montgomery Ward, and J. C. Penney, had resisted third-party credit companies from the outset. As the universal cards grew in size, however, smaller retailers found them appealing. Small retailers were precluded from running their own credit operations because of the high costs; since they catered to a clientele that bought many consumer goods on credit, it made sense for them to accept third-party cards. Furthermore, many small retailers, particularly the specialty stores, had little need to ensure the loyalty of customers who visited their shops only occasionally.

Despite the inroads the third-party cards made into the ranks of the smaller retailers in the early 1970s, they still could not gain access to the larger stores. National chains such as J. C. Penney and Sears continued to operate their own credit card plans. Regional retailers, meanwhile, joined together to pool their credit operations, using an outside credit management company to handle all of the transactions. Although more expensive than allowing the use of third-party cards, private-label card operations had the singular advantage of maintaining the retailer's identity and its relationship with its customers.

The breakthrough for the bank cards finally came in 1979 when J. C. Penney stunned the industry by signing an agreement with Visa. Although Penney had been an early and vocal opponent of third-party credit cards, its change of heart can be explained by the tremendous competitive jump it gained on the other large retailers, as well as by the favorable discount rate it received from Visa.

While Penney's move prompted some of the other major retailers to begin accepting third-party cards, the bank cards did not receive the tremendous windfall they had expected, nor did it have the deleterious effect upon the retailers' credit card operations that many had predicted. The more favorable conditions and the lack of an annual fee for the retailers' cards continued to make them an attractive alternative to third-party cards. Furthermore, many retailers continued to refuse bank cards or accepted them only at a limited number of stores. Two years after the Penney-Visa agreement, less than half of the country's major retailers accepted third-party bank cards.

The agreement's main beneficiary among the third-party cards appeared to be American Express. Since only a small percentage of the department stores' regular customers carried American Express cards, the retailers were not as fearful as they were with the bank cards, of having their customers discard the store credit card in favor of the American Express card. Furthermore, by accepting the T&E cards, they were able to attract many T&E cardholders who traveled into their region on business or vacation. Significantly more affluent than the average bank cardholder, this group was also more likely to make high-margin impulse purchases. By the early 1980s, American Express cards were welcomed at three-quarters of the nation's department stores.

Throughout the 1970s and into the 1980s, the bank card companies grew at a much faster pace than any other segment of the credit card industry. However, despite ever increasing billings, more and more cardholders, and a growing number of merchants, the companies remained only marginally profitable. The banks' credit card operations consistently lagged far behind every other area of their operations. From 1979 to 1981, as the cost of money skyrocketed during the inflationary Carter years, the banks actually lost money on their credit cards.

In contrast, the T&E card companies generated substantial profits for a number of years, owing in large part to their more affluent cardholder base—which produced account interest revenues and fewer losses due to fraud or default—and their annual fee. Neither of these advantages accrued to the bank card companies. Achieving a large cardholder base meant accepting customers with a lower economic profile, while market pressures prevented them from instituting an annual fee.

From the outset, the bank card companies had to scramble even to approach profitability. Faced with the huge startup costs of developing a nationwide credit card operation, the banks needed to acquire large customer bases quickly. Mass mailings of unsolicited cards accomplished this, but they also left the companies open to large losses due to fraud, which diluted profits. Processing problems also ate into revenues. Early processing systems were overwhelmed by the huge increases in charge slips and accounts following the mass mailings. Not until 1976 were the credit card companies able to abandon the cumbersome and inefficient "country club" billing system, which required the companies to return each charge slip to the customer.

While they worked to control costs, the banks also struggled to maximize their revenue. One method focused on the calculation of finance charges. Prevented from raising the actual finance charge by restrictive usury laws, the banks instead altered their methods of calculating interest charges, moving from the adjusted balance method, which calculated interest on the balance at the time payment was due, to the average daily balance system, which assessed interest from the date a charge was made. Other methods of increasing revenues included marketing various products and services, such as insurance, with monthly statements; bundling a number of bank services, such as checking and check-cashing cards, along with the credit card and marketing the complete package to customers; selling customer lists to mailing houses, a practice that was eventually outlawed; and marketing return envelopes to advertisers.

All of these efforts increased revenues, but never enough to move the banks more than marginally into the black. The key to achieving significant profits was the imposition of an annual fee for cardholders. Many banks had recognized the need for an annual fee as far back as 1970. However, unlike T&E card companies, which had begun charging their cardholders an annual fee in the 1950s, they had refrained from imposing such a fee because of market pressures. No bank was willing to lose market share by being the first to impose an annual fee.

The banks had hoped to offset the lack of an annual fee by charging interest on unpaid balances. But they were hampered in doing so by usury laws, which placed a ceiling on interest rates, and by the tendency of the vast majority of cardholders to pay off their bills on time, denying the company any interest charges. In 1976, Citibank attempted to solve the problem of paid-up accounts by imposing a monthly 50-cent fee on such accounts. This ill-conceived plan drew cries of outrage from the public and censure from Congress and seemed to bear out the prevailing wisdom on the inadvisability of imposing an annual fee.

As the decade drew to a close, events finally began to turn in favor of the bank card companies. As rising interest rates squeezed many companies, states finally agreed to ease or eliminate restrictive usury ceilings, allowing the banks to raise their interest rates. Their good fortune continued in 1980 when President Jimmy Carter conveniently provided the pretext for initiating an industrywide move to annual fees. In an attempt to curb inflation, he announced new rules mandating the creation by credit card issuers of a non-interest-bearing reserve from all new consumer credit extended after 14 March 1980. In response, a number of banks announced the imposition of an annual fee to cover this government-enforced loss of revenue. The bank card companies expected this move to cost them a significant portion of their cardholder base, but contrary to earlier fears, the mass exodus of customers never materialized. The relatively small decrease in the companies' cardholder base was more than offset by the increased revenue from the fees. More importantly, the annual fee, coupled with the easing of interest rates, allowed the companies to return to profitability.

The events of 1981 marked the beginning of a period of tremendous growth for the credit card industry, in both profits and cardholders. From 1982 to 1986, profits soared as bank card operations outperformed every other form of bank debt, both because of the imposition of the annual fee and because of the wide spread between credit card finance charges and prevailing interest rates. As rates dropped in the early 1980s, banks chose not to drop their finance charge rates with them. They judged the public to be relatively insensitive to high interest rates on credit cards. Their asssessment was based on the tremendous growth in the use of the credit card as a vehicle for consumer credit. Events subsequently bore out their conclusions. More recently, their unwillingness to lower interest rates has aroused considerable opposition from consumers' rights organizations. Thus far, however, most efforts to legislate limits on credit card interest rates have been stopped by the industry's powerful lobby.

The number of cardholders and participating banks rose in an equally precipitous manner. By 1986, more than 55 percent of all families possessed a bank card—more than three times the number for 1970. The number of participating banks had climbed from 71 to 90 percent. All of this growth meant that the "easy" customers had been signed up. Marketing efforts would now be focused on attracting the few remaining consumers who did not have a card, as well as luring those who did away from rival companies.

One of the most effective of these marketing techniques has been the affinity card program. Begun in 1985 by both Visa and MasterCard, affinity cards have spread throughout the industry. There are three basic types of affinity cards: product benefit cards, which provide users with various types of bonuses for usage; lifestyle cards, which are marketed to people with a particular interest, often a charitable cause, and which provide the charity with some form of remuneration for the use of the cards; and personality cards, which have sought to cash in on the public's fascination with certain individuals, such as Elvis Presley. After a very successful period, affinity card programs are becoming much more difficult to market because numerous competitors have jumped onto the bandwagon in recent years.

Credit card companies have also intensified their competition for market share at both the bottom and top ends of the market. On the low end, a number of banks have introduced secured credit card programs to increase their cardholder base. Marketed to customers who have a lower income or poor credit records, secured credit cards require the cardholder to maintain an account at the bank, which is then used to "secure" that person's credit. The upper limit on such credit cards is usually tied to the size of the initial deposit, which is held by the bank as collateral should the cardholder fail to make payments on his or her outstanding credit.

A much more lucrative and more competitive campaign has been waged by the credit card companies for the high end of the marketplace. The attraction of this segment of the marketplace is obvious—high-end customers generally have higher monthly bills and are significantly lower credit risks. Throughout the 1970s, the prestige card field, as it was called, was dominated by the T&E industry. American Express, with its gold card, Diners Club, and Carte Blanche were the primary contenders. In the early 1980s, however, both Visa and MasterCard introduced their own prestige cards and very quickly established themselves as serious competitors, surpassing both Diners Club and Carte Blanche and rivaling American Express for the top spot. American Express responded to this incursion into its territory with the introduction of the Optima card in 1988. Unlike the gold card, which used the banks to provide the revolving credit, Optima has its credit supplied directly by American Express, completely bypassing the banks.

In addition to these marketing campaigns, the banks have sought to increase their profits through their continuing efforts to lower operational costs and to introduce new sources of revenue. On the cost side of the balance sheet, banks have invested considerable capital and time in lowering processing costs. Many, particularly smaller banks, have contracted their operations out to third parties. For the moment, this alternative has been attractive because intense competition among third-party operators has kept rates low. Larger banks have kept charge of their own operations so that they can better integrate them with other bank services to their customers. In an effort to cut costs, some larger banks have moved their processing operations to out-of-state locations that offer lower rents and cheaper labor.

On the revenue side, banks have been much more successful at increasing interest revenues. A significant development has been the introduction of securitization, which involves the bundling and sale of credit card receivables to investors in the form of securities. Offered as low-risk, fixed-rate investments, these securities have allowed the bank card companies to lower the cost of funds in relation to the interest charged to cardholders, thereby increasing profits.

In addition to the increased competition among existing credit card companies, the 1980s have also seen the introduction of a new major competitor—the Discover card. Launched in 1986 by Sears, the Discover card was intended to be the culmination of the retail giant's expansion into financial services. Following its acquisition of the Coldwell Banker real estate company and the Dean Witter brokerage company in the 1980s, Sears was looking for another opportunity to expand its financial services. Already the largest issuer of credit cards in the world through its retail operations, it decided to launch a universal credit card.

When Sears chose to begin marketing the card, credit card profits were at an all-time high. Unfortunately for Sears, the industry was also near its saturation point. While Discover has managed to achieve a considerable cardholder base, it has operated solidly in the red for most of its short history. Furthermore, it still trails its major competitors—Visa and MasterCard—by a considerable margin, both in charge volume and in number of cards in circulation. Obviously, Discover could not hope to overtake its rivals overnight, and not without considerable losses. However, it remains to be seen whether it will ultimately prove to be a profitable venture for Sears.

Just as the 1980s have been boom years for the credit card industry, they have also witnessed the steady growth of an industry that many believe will eventually replace the credit card—electronic funds transfer (EFT) systems. EFT is a logical extension of the credit card. Just as the credit card sought to facilitate transactions between merchants and customers by eliminating the need for cash, EFT systems are trying to go a step further by eliminating the middleman: it electronically debits the customer's account and credits the same amount to the merchant's account through point-of-sale (POS) terminals.

This is the long-term direction of many EFT systems. In the interim, however, a number of other EFT systems have been developed to meet other specific needs. These include ATMs and a variety of systems that operate over telephone lines on-line to computers.

The era of electronic funds transfer began in the United States in 1969 with the installation of the first Docutel cash dispenser machines. This machine was activated by a credit card to which a magnetic stripe had been affixed. To expand the market for the machines to include customers who did not, would not, or could not own a credit card, banks developed special debit cards that would give these customers access to the machines.

The cash dispenser field received a welcome boost from American Express in 1975 when it decided to add a magnetic Docutel strip to the back of its prestigious gold card, which was thus converted into a debit as well as a credit card. American Express also experimented with using the machines in airports to dispense traveler's checks rather than cash. Citibank, which was moving into competition with American Express in the traveler's check business, soon introduced its own line of dispenser machines.

The growing use of cash dispensers and the new ATMs created a demand for a national network that would allow consumers to obtain cash across the country. Both Visa and MasterCard had planned for the advent of nationwide networking for years. Their plans were preempted, however, by the banks. Having recognized their earlier mistake in ceding control of the credit card field to Visa and MasterCard, various banks and banking consortiums began forming their own nationwide networks of ATMs in the late 1970s and early 1980s. Although these networks could be used by the Visa and MasterCard cardholders, they were owned and operated by the banks, not the credit card companies. (Both Visa and MasterCard have moved to acquire these systems in the 1980s and now control a significant portion of the national ATM networks.)

Like the credit card, cash dispensers and debit cards also enjoyed widespread use internationally. For many European credit companies debit cards constituted a major portion of their business. For example, Carte Bleue, the largest French credit card company, issued 60 percent more debit cards than Visa cards in 1977. Debit cards were also popular in Great Britain and, in particular, Japan. By 1978, Japan was the world's leader in the number of debit cards, electronic banking machines, cash dispensers, automated depositors, and ATMs. Debit cards outnumbered credit cards in Japan by more than seven million, or 20 percent.

In the United States, most EFT systems operated on-line to central mainframe computers, creating very secure but expensive systems. In 1979, the forty-two largest banks in Switzerland implemented an ATM network of specially modified Dassault machines that could be polled periodically. These banks thus combined the economy of an off-line system with the security of an on-line one. Fraud losses were further minimized by a $100 per day per customer limit on withdrawals.

ATMs continued to proliferate throughout the world during the 1980s. As competition for ATM customers has increased, banks have now begun offering more sophisticated machines that can perform a much wider array of services without the need for human intervention. Banks have also begun to charge customers for usage of the machines, having recognized the potential of ATMs as another profit center for their operations.

While ATMs and cash dispensers have been quite successful and well received by the public, other forms of electronic funds transfer have yet to achieve widespread acceptance. Telephone bill payments and the associated telephone transaction system, home banking through two-way cable systems, and linkups with home computers continue to offer tremendous potential but have failed to catch on. Point-of-sale networks have been particularly disappointing. Unlike debit cards, such as those used in ATMs, which simply debit the account of the user, POS cards both debit the customer's account and credit those funds to the merchant's account. Despite the potential of POS networks, they have yet to be employed extensively, partly because of the industry's failure to agree upon a standard. The major impediment has been the fantastic cost of placing every merchant and every bank in the country on-line, which a full-scale POS network would require. Until the logistical and technological problems can be solved and a solution agreed upon by the industry, POS cards will remain only a limited application. Nevertheless, it is only a matter of time before the credit card industry is profoundly affected by this and other EFT systems.

1

Diners Club: The Birth of an Industry

IN 1949, AS THE LUNCHEON TABLES WERE cleared at Major's Cabin Grill, a popular New York restaurant of the period whose location next door to the Empire State Building was then a considerable asset, three men sat huddled over a prime table off to one side. One of them was a tall, former Ivy League football player named Alfred Bloomingdale, a grandson of the founder of the posh Bloomingdale store. The other two were Frank McNamara, an old friend of Bloomingdale's, and McNamara's attorney, Ralph Snyder.

Bloomingdale, a former producer of Broadway shows, was in the midst of an unsuccessful stint as a film producer in Hollywood. He was back in New York on one of his frequent trips to visit his ailing father, who had been hospitalized since 1947 and was in steady decline. It was while he was waiting to visit his father at Scofield Hospital that Bloomingdale ran into his friend Frank McNamara, who invited him to lunch. Looking for a way to take his mind off of his father's illness, Bloomingdale accepted.

Francis X. McNamara, later described by Bloomingdale as "one of the great salesmen of all times," was then head of an unsuccessful finance company, the Hamilton Credit Corporation. According to Bloomingdale, Hamilton Credit at that time had $35,000 of uncollected and probably uncollectable receivables and little more, which gave McNamara the time to have long luncheons with his friends. Possibly because of his frequent involvement in litigation, McNamara was operating his company out of the office of his attorney, Ralph Snyder, who gave him the use of a desk.

The topic of conversation on this historic day was McNamara's difficulty in collecting one of his debts. One of McNamara's clients, who operated a business in the Bronx, lent his charge accounts to his neighbors. If one of his poor neighbors needed a prescription in the middle of the night, this entrepreneur would tell the neighbor to go to a particular drugstore and use his charge account, which he would okay over the phone. If the prescription were, say, $30, he would then charge the neighbor $40 and collect it over time.

While the components of this transaction were hardly novel—both charge accounts and installment credit were widespread—the involvement of a middleman, who used his own creditworthiness to obtain credit from a store, extend that credit to an individual who might not otherwise be able to obtain it, and then collect the principal and interest from the party who had needed the credit, was an intriguing twist on the normal process of extending credit. However, as this entrepreneur soon discovered, such an arrangement worked on a limited scale but was not possible on a widespread basis without the infusion of additional capital.

Since stores did not typically charge interest to their charge account customers in those days, customers were expected to clear up their outstanding charges within the reasonable period of time to keep their credit from being cut off. And yet the poor individuals who were forced to use the services of the Bronx businessman for their credit sometimes had great difficulty paying off the credit within a short period of time. For this reason, Hamilton Credit had lent the fellow $3,000, and by the time of the luncheon, McNamara desperately needed his capital back.

McNamara presented his dilemma to his two friends. The three men kicked around the idea of lending "charge-plates" to others as a way of facilitating Hamilton Credit's efforts to extend credit. Charga-plates were a type of credit card that many larger retailers offered to their customers. The main purpose of the plates, aside from extending credit, was to help the clerks identify customers. In appearance, charga-plates were small metal tags with indented letters and numbers, resembling in size and form the "dog tags" worn by soldiers and civilians during the war and for some time afterwards. The cards were inserted into a machine with a carbon paper on top and a roller was passed over them, making an impression in a manner similar to what is done today with plastic credit cards. Perhaps because they were sitting in a restaurant at the time, the thought hit the three men that charga-plates would work best in restaurants.

In discussing the overall concept, the three men found two flaws in the operation of McNamara's Bronx customer. First, he was lending the money to the wrong people. Poor people obviously are in need of credit but are least able to repay it on a timely basis. Bloomingdale, who had spent time in the family store, was quite aware of this problem. Second, the operator had to wait for an emergency before a customer used his service. An operation depending on sporadic and unpredictable use could hardly succeed unless it had a huge customer base. One of the three founders of the Diners Club remarked that, in contrast, within a mile of where they sat were all of the important restaurants of New York, every one of which offered charge accounts to its regular customers. Bloomingdale, in fact, had charge accounts at "21" and most of the other important restaurants in the vicinity. Restaurants, it would appear, were the ideal market.

In their excitement, they called over Major, the proprietor, and asked him how much he would pay for business that he would not ordinarily get. Without flinching, Major replied, "7 percent," a number that established a major industry and persevered as the industry standard for several decades. Sometime later, when these three young entrepreneurs were well established, they had occasion to ask Major how he came up with the famous 7 percent. He answered, "A travel agent would have charged 10 percent."

As mentioned earlier, both McNamara and Bloomingdale had had credit experience, McNamara through his Bronx connection and Bloomingdale through his experience in the family store. They knew, for example, that several stores had charga-plates that could be used at more than one store. They also knew of the gasoline cards that had been around for decades. However, the gasoline companies issued credit cards to stimulate sales of gasoline, and the stores issued charga-plates to stimulate sales of their merchandise. When stores accepted other stores' charga-plates, it was done without fee on an exchange basis only.

The critical concept in this new business they were contemplating was the notion of having a third party serve as an intermediary between the grantors of credit and those who used the credit. And the discount, Major's 7 percent, would be the means of paying for the operation. As the result of their luncheon, the three men decided to set up a small business to test their idea. They perceived the primary market to be salesmen traveling around New York who would probably want a way to charge their meals. Since these salesmen were charged nothing for the card (the concept of an annual fee came some years later), many of them signed up. Thus was Diners Club born.

To bankroll the new enterprise, McNamara contributed Hamilton

Credit and its $35,000 in uncollectable receivables, and Bloomingdale put up $5,000 in cash. That $5,000 was the only money that the new company, begun within the folds of the Hamilton Credit Corporation, actually had. But McNamara was able to go to the bank with the $5,000 and the $35,000 in receivables and borrow $35,000 to get the enterprise off the ground. Shortly after that luncheon, Bloomingdale went back to California with a note in his pocket for $5,000 and an equity position in the new enterprise. Although he was personally intrigued by the idea, Bloomingdale had lent the money to McNamara more out of friendship than in hopes of beginning a profitable venture.

After Bloomingdale went back to California, McNamara and Snyder lost no time in launching the new enterprise from their office in New York's Empire State Building. Their initial marketing approach was both simple and inexpensive—they distributed leaflets advertising their new card under the doors of offices in the Empire State Building. The card was free, and they did not check anyone's credit. Since they were located in the Empire State Building, interested persons would come to their office, giving McNamara and Snyder an opportunity to look them over. If they looked trustworthy and claimed to have a job, they were given a card. At about the same time, McNamara and Snyder signed up ten or twelve restaurants around the Empire State Building to handle the first customers.

During the first month of operation, the new company did $2,000 in business, which produced a new income of 7 percent, or $140. During the second month, the business grew even more rapidly, and McNamara and Snyder needed additional capital. When they contacted their friend Bloomingdale, he said he would advance additional funds only if he could have a sizable interest in the firm, but the two New York entrepreneurs, confident of the eventual success of their enterprise, would not agree to give up substantial ownership. As a result, Bloomingdale began his own credit card operation in Los Angeles, known as Dine and Sign.

Following the pattern established by McNamara and Snyder on the other coast, Bloomingdale signed up twenty-five restaurants in Los Angeles. Within three months, he was up to about $150,000 a month in business, but was out of capital because he had no substantial sources of credit himself. By this time, his friends in New York were doing about $250,000 a month, so the three decided to merge their operation under the assumption, according to Bloomingdale, that "if they were all going to go broke, they might as well do it together." Thus, within three months of starting up, the Diners Club operation was "nationwide," operating in both New York City and Los Angeles. Shortly thereafter, they expanded their operation into Boston when they bought out a similar operation that had been started by one of Bloomingdale's former partners in his Dine and Sign business.

In its first year of operation, Diners Club was 70 percent owned by McNamara, with the remaining 30 percent equally owned by Bloomingdale and Snyder. When they merged, the operation became known as Diners Club everywhere. By that point, Bloomingdale had loaned the operation an additional $25,000, which, added to the original $5,000 and the small amount used to begin Dine and Sign, turned out to be the only money he ever put in the business.

Since a credit card operation needs a sizable amount of its own credit to extend to its customers, the three partners spent a great deal of their time in search of new sources of credit. One of the most successful and least expensive ways of financing the operation was through a discovery that Bloomingdale made, known to later generations of scholars and corporate treasurers as "float." Since the corporation had offices in New York and Los Angeles, New York bills were paid with checks drawn on a bank account in Los Angeles, which took several days to clear. This ingenious operation produced free credit for many years until, according to Bloomingdale, "one time a bank merged with helicopter and all my checks bounced." When faster methods of check clearing came into widespread use, the value of that method was greatly diminished.

As the business grew larger, and as the need for credit became more intense, the partners came up with a number of other innovations to obtain credit at no cost to themselves. One method involved the timing of the bills they had to pay to restaurants and the bills their customers had to pay to them. Their agreement with the restaurants was that Diners Club could have thirty-day trade credit for the bills accumulated during a month. Thus, they found that if they could get their customers to pay for all of a month's charges at the end of the month, they could maximize the size of the customer payment, as well as obtain at least a month's free float from the restaurants. In the early days of credit cards, virtually all cardholders paid their bills on time. Thus, on the average, they were indeed provided with thirty days of free float.

Of course, other problems, some of which still plague the industry, began to emerge. For example, some customers did not pay their bills on time. When Bloomingdale started Dine and Sign in Los Angeles, he issued 20,000 cards. However, his staff could not tell from the charge slips who was charging because the signature frequently bore no resemblance to the name. So Bloomingdale was forced to hire handwriting experts who examined voting records to try to find out who was using the cards. He discovered that when a card was free, the issuer did not know who would use the card. And since it was important to have widespread distribution to launch the credit card program, individuals were not charged for membership and were sent unsolicited cards through the mail. Bloomingdale bought a list of Cadillac owners, for example, all of whom were mailed free Dine and Sign cards. The credit card was so new that recipients thought it was a gag and started using them to "play along." Some of them lent the cards out to their friends, creating additional problems.

The early Diners Club credit cards were not credit cards at all; they were in fact credit "books." Since the "card" holders had to know where these instruments could be used, they were sent miniature books with a paper credit card and a signature on the front and a list of establishments within. In fact, to publicize the names of new restaurants accepting the cards, the operation was forced to begin a periodic magazine, which became a familiar feature of later credit card companies.

In the formative years, Diners Club had no limit on the amount that cardholders could spend. There were also no "hot lists" of stolen or "runaway" cards that had greatly exceeded their credit limits. So few places were using the cards that Diners Club could call and ask that a list be posted next to the cash register, indicating which cards were not to be honored. The partners soon found out that a person who was "on the lam" with a card would only go to the best places. He never went to Joe's Beanery, only to Romanoff's. So they would call Romanoff's and catch him most of the time. They hired their own detective, who arrested the malefactors or at least recovered the credit cards.

In 1950, after a year of phenomenal growth and the loss of some $300,000, Frank McNamara decided that he wanted to get out of the business. He did not think there was anything in it beyond restaurants and the salesmen who ate in them. Opting instead for the housing business, he sold his 70 percent interest in Diners Club to Bloomingdale and Snyder so that each of them would have 50 percent. The cost was $250,000, and Bloomingdale and Snyder each borrowed $125,000 from the bank.

Although the two partners could borrow money on their personal signatures and collateral, no bank was willing to extend the credit needed by the corporation. Therefore, in its first year of operation, the company was forced to use a "factor" to whom Diners Club sold its accounts receivable at a discount, Following the loss of $300,000 in 1950, the company struggled for a year and a half before returning to profitability. It was then able to obtain credit, first from a small bank named Sterling Bank and later, when the company became much more successful, from the larger banks, which began to compete for the privilege of lending it money. Diners Club would continue to turn a profit for the next eighteen years until control was purchased by Continental in 1970.

By the late 1950s, Diners Club was opening offices in major cities throughout the United States, and in 1951 it went international. Since it had very little capital at that time, rather than open offices in other countries the company sold franchises to the Diners Club name and operating system. The first three franchises were sold outright; the partners retained a 25 percent interest in all subsequent ones.

The first Diners Club franchise, which opened in England, literally came to them. A British citizen on the American lecture circuit became intrigued by the Diners Club idea. When he approached the company and asked whether he could start it in England, he was given the go-ahead. Thereafter, they merely exchanged charges, with no franchise fee or other payment coming to Diners Club. Later on, they concluded a more formal agreement, and eventually the American Diners Club owned 50 percent and one share.

Diners Club did not remain exclusively in the restaurant business for long. The partners pioneered the use of their card in hotels, retail stores, and virtually every line of business in which credit cards came to be used in later years. In addition, they used the direct mail contact they had with their customers to sell insurance and other merchandise, a practice that has, if anything, intensified over time.

Within the next four years, the now worldwide company had grown to such an extent that a further influx of equity was needed, forcing the company to go public. Bloomingdale and Snyder each held onto approximately 30 percent of the shares, releasing 40 percent for public distribution.

In its formative years, Diners Club sales representatives occasionally gave merchants exclusive rights to accept the card within a particular area. The practice of extending exclusivity lasted for only a few years before its limitations and complexity became apparent. Thereafter, Diners Club representatives were dispatched to sign up business.

Certain industries resisted. The airlines, which had their own credit card plan, mounted a nearly united front to keep out third-party credit card companies for many years. Diners Club broke through when it signed Western Airlines, the first airline to accept outside credit cards. Western was signed because of Bloomingdale's personal friendship with the officers of the airline. Ironically, the resistance was strongest from the large retailers. Bloomingdale was not even able to sign up Bloomingdale's, although by that time it was no longer owned by the family.

As the business expanded in many different lines, it was forced to become more flexible. The 7 percent standard suggested by Major was soon dropped by the wayside as a varying discount rate was applied based upon the size of the average charge. Since the cost of handling a credit card slip did not change with the size of the slip, the company could afford to offer lower discounts to some clients—for example, to the airlines, whose average charge was so large. Thus, the airlines, which today are typically charged a discount of only about one percent, were given a discount of 3 percent, while the restaurants' charge remained at 7 percent.

Although Diners Club wanted to also sign up gas stations to increase the usefulness of the card, the very low average charge for a gasoline transaction would have necessitated a restaurant-sized discount of at least 7 percent, which would have been too high to attract much interest in the often price-competitive gasoline business.

Eventually, the 7 percent standard had to be abandoned, even for restaurants. Although the company tried very hard to maintain a uniform discount for restaurants, in order to not favor one over another, it was forced to break that rule when it began to sign up restaurant chains. In addition, Diners Club was not able to maintain its policy of paying only once a month when the credit volume from restaurants grew extremely large. In places like New York, the company often had to pay twice or three times a month, although it maintained its once-a-month payment policy in more rural areas.

In the early years of the Diners Club operation, new ideas and innovations flew about at a rapid pace, and nearly every aspect of today's credit card business that was technologically feasible was tried. Not only did Diners Club sell insurance using the card, but loans of up to $25,000 were made on it.

Additional technical staff were added as the operation grew in size and complexity. A young commercial artist named Spencer Nilson (who later started the *Nilson Report*, the leading credit card newsletter) took over promotion, advertising, and direct-mail operations. A few ideas failed; the attempt to sell mutual funds on credit cards, for instance, failed at least partly because of government disapproval. But many more ideas proved successful.

As might be expected in an innovative and rapidly expanding business, tension was high and battles were fought almost daily. Early on, when it was questionable from one day to the next whether Diners Club could stay afloat, the company was faced with the realization that if it failed, it could take with it 100–200 of the best restaurants in America.

As Diners Club entered a new city to sign up merchants, the local better business bureau would view it with great suspicion. In addition, a number of trade associations tried to prevent its widespread adoption.

The company was resisted by the American Hotel Association for many years until it got into its first hotel, and then it had to do battle with the florists. Each battle was unique, and victory was often achieved only through the most ingenious methods.

For example, the restaurant association in the state of Washington attempted to keep out Diners Club by having association members agree to not accept the card. Bloomingdale broke that boycott through the extreme method of starting his own restaurant in downtown Seattle. Since his was the only restaurant that would accept Diners Club, cardholding businesspeople who happened to be in Seattle would flock to it. Pretty soon, the other downtown restaurants that were dependent on the patronage of traveling businesspeople gave in, and Washington became an open state.

The Diners Club monopoly in the T&E business lasted for only about seven years. Its success attracted imitators American Express and Carte Blanche, which launched their own T&E cards. Banks also began offering T&E cards. In spite of the competition, Diners Club continued to thrive through the 1950s. However, it would soon relinquish its leadership in the industry, signaling the beginning of a new phase in the development of the modern credit card industry. Diners Club's ability to overcome the various initial obstacles facing third-party credit cards had convinced a number of companies that the concept could and would work. The market existed. What was needed was a way to streamline and extend operations to prepare for the establishment of a coordinated, worldwide network. As difficult as it would be to reach that point, the nascent industry now had a successful example to guide it.

When Bloomingdale's partner Ralph Snyder died in the late 1950s, his shares were passed on to his family, leaving Bloomingdale as the only founder still with the company. Unable to secure the necessary capital to purchase Snyder's shares on his own, Bloomingdale contacted several friends at Continental Insurance Company and negotiated Continental's acquisition of the shares from Snyder's family.

The sale of these shares to Continental was not the only attempt to sell the company. In 1965, Diners Club had engaged in merger discussions with J. C. Penney. Simultaneously, it also contacted Chase Manhattan Bank, which eventually agreed to purchase the company for $56.6 million. A memo of intent was signed in November, and everything seemed to be moving ahead smoothly. However, the following year the Justice Department ended the acquisition by judging that it would violate antitrust laws.

The Continental sale seemed to be just what Bloomingdale wanted.

But within a few years, he began to find himself at odds with his new colleagues. In 1966, Continental had gained its first seat on the board of directors. The following year, it added two more seats as it continued to purchase convertible debentures, which increased its stock position in the company. These new directors soon began to argue with Bloomingdale over the management of Diners Club. A two-year struggle for control of the company ensued.

Inevitably, the internal strife took its toll on Diners Club's performance. In 1968, Diners Club earned a healthy $2.4 million. But the following year, reeling from the increased competition of American Express and the new bank cards, BankAmericard and Master Charge, the company's profits plummeted to just over $900,000. Bloomingdale was forced to resign as head of the company. Since Continental did not want Bloomingdale competing with it by going to American Express or Carte Blanche, it gave him a lifetime contract. The following year, Continental completed its acquisition of the company when it issued a successful tender offer for the remaining two-thirds of Diners Club shares.

Bloomingdale would remain with the company, at least in name, and retain a small stock position in it until his death in 1981. By then, Diners Club had been purchased by Citibank (in 1980), which had also purchased Carte Blanche a few years earlier. Today, Diners Club continues to operate as a profitable subsidiary of the New York banking giant. However, its relatively small place in today's credit card marketplace gives little indication of its status as the pioneer of the modern credit card industry. As for Alfred Bloomingdale, Frank McNamara, and Ralph Snyder, their contributions to the credit card industry have largely been forgotten, which is not surprising. In sharp contrast with industries such as auto manufacturing, where executives and innovators have always held center stage, the credit card industry has always been and continues to be largely a faceless one, with few people ever holding the spotlight for more than a few moments.

2

The History of Credit

DINERS CLUB WAS THE FIRST MODERN credit card. Yet the basic concepts underlying the new industry had been in existence for some time. In fact, the credit card has been with us, with minor changes, for nearly the entire twentieth century. The founders of Diners Club introduced no radically new ideas. Rather, they combined a number of well-known and widely used techniques for extending credit and changed the way credit service was delivered to the consumer. The key to their success was their recognition of the need and untapped demand for a mobile credit vehicle, coupled with their ability and foresight in turning that realization into a viable and profitable enterprise.

Innovations in the credit card industry have developed slowly and have generally conformed to the expressed needs of society. Little of the sophisticated technology currently used in the credit card industry, such as switching networks, computer authorization, and satellite transmission, was developed specifically for it. Existing technology has usually been adapted to fit the needs of the developing industry.

It is also important to remember that the credit card industry developed almost entirely as an American innovation designed to fit certain economic, social, and technological characteristics of this country. Even today, much of the worldwide credit card industry is still controlled by American companies and their subsidiaries or licensees.

In the United States, the primary reason for the success of the credit card has been its credit feature rather than its convenience. When

I asked a representative cross-section of American families in a 1970 survey (conducted through the auspices of the Survey Research Center of the University of Michigan and published in 1972 as *Credit Card Use in the United States*) what they considered the advantages of credit card use, the largest proportion responded that credit cards enabled them to buy without having the cash. This response was common among both users and nonusers of credit cards. The survey also revealed that it was only among higher income families that the credit function of credit cards was not a primary factor motivating their use.

The credit use of credit cards has also been of paramount importance to card issuers, particularly banks, which have charged a low annual fee (or no fee at all) and depended upon interest charges for up to two-thirds of their total revenue. It is not difficult to see why the credit card industry has flourished in the United States, where consumer credit has always been looked upon much more favorably and, consequently, has been used much more extensively than in other countries.

The Early Development of Credit

In tracing the development of the credit card industry, one must begin with a history of credit itself. According to economic anthropologists, the use of credit predates even the use of money. Historian Paul Einzig wrote in *Primitive Money* that "credit existed on a fairly extensive scale long before the state of money economy was reached." A person might borrow seed to be repaid from the next harvested crop, or to pay for such things as ransom fines and bribe money and to carry on trade.

Even the earliest recorded documents carry references to credit. The Code of Hammurabi, written in Babylonia about 1750 B.C., mentions one of the earliest restrictions on credit: "If a man be in debt and sell his wife, son, or daughter or bind them over to service for three years, they shall work in the house of their purchaser or master; in the fourth year they shall be given their freedom." There are also many references to credit in the Old Testament, usually in connection with the sin of usury. For example, Leviticus 25:37 states, "Thou shalt not give him thy money upon usury, nor lend him thy victuals for increase."

It is clear, from these and other examples, that ever since the introduction of the concept of credit, strong moral forces were set against the consumer loan. In times of subsistence, when most persons borrowed only to stay alive, it is not difficult to understand why profiting at the expense of someone else's misery was thought to be morally reprehensible. But the moral force of early prohibitions against usury has remained with us even in the age of affluence, when consumer borrowing has motivations other than subsistence. According to Charles Hardy, author of *Consumer Credit and Its Uses*, "The significant thing to observe is that there was in these early days no clear idea of that which, today, we call capital. For the most part, loans were not made to persons, who because they borrowed, were able to increase their own earning power and through this increase repay their debts."

The Greeks and Romans were especially prejudiced against the taking of interest. The Greek philosophers, Plato and Aristotle, both condemned interest; Aristotle's arguments, in particular, influenced the thinking of the Roman Catholic church for well over a thousand years. The Romans, however, distinguished between productive credit, which was used for business and investment, and consumptive credit, which involved personal loans for purposes of consumption, often for borrowers on the verge of starvation. As industry and commerce played a larger and larger role in Roman society, many of the restrictions broke down; Justinian's Code in the sixth century recognized interest and set maximum legal rates for various types of loans. (The notion of maximum legal rates continues to plague the credit card industry some fifteen hundred years after Justinian.)

In the early Middle Ages, the halting of commerce combined with the increasing influence of the Roman Catholic Church ended most types of lending. During this period, money lending was left to the Jews, who were outside the Church's jurisdiction. Toward the end of this period, however, trade resumed and credit became relatively widespread. Historian Herbert Heaton could be describing the late twentieth century when he says of this period, in his book *Economic History of Europe*, that cash on delivery was relatively rare, lending and borrowing were pervasive, and the debtor-creditor relationship was found in all classes from peasant to pope. Loans of all kinds—short-, medium-, and long-term—were common. Consumption loans were used to purchase food, clothing, or luxuries, while capital loans were used to finance production or trade.

The Protestant Reformation hastened the decline of usury prohibition by breaking Europe into independent religious units. The usury question could then be settled on a country-by-country basis, as well as brought from the religious into the secular arena. In 1545, England replaced the prohibition on interest with a maximum interest rate. By the eighteenth century, maximum rate laws had replaced the prohibition against interest in all of the western European countries.

The pendulum was to swing still further toward the liberalization of the use of credit in nineteenth-century England, where the great liberal economists, Adam Smith, David Ricardo, and John Stuart Mill, argued against restrictions on the rate of interest, predating the conservative economists who make the same arguments in our own day. In 1854, England removed all restrictions on the rate of interest, and within a few years, Germany, Holland, and Belgium all followed its example. As so often happens, however, the pendulum began to swing back over the next fifty years toward a more restrictive view of the use of credit, and by the year 1900, all of the western European nations again had legal limitations on interest charges. Even with this retrenchment, however, the use of credit at the beginning of the twentieth century was more widespread than it had been one hundred years earlier.

Credit in the United States

In the United States, nearly all of the states ignored the liberal examples of their ancestral countries in Europe and retained interest rate ceilings from the moment they achieved statehood. (The existence of such ceilings in almost all states helps explain why usury laws have been more of a problem for the credit card industry in the United States than in Europe.) But despite that limitation, the general use of credit in the fledgling nation was widespread. In fact, there is little, if any, difference between the way credit is used in the United States today and the way it was used in the early 1800s, with the single exception of technology.

Records indicate that both installment credit and a form of revolving credit were widespread in the early days of the Republic. Economist Rolf Nugent noted, in *Consumer Credit and Economic Stability*, that "in rural areas, horses, plows, carriages, seed, clocks, and household furniture were frequently sold for promissory notes payable after the harvest." Installment sales were commonplace in urban areas, particularly for high-priced durable goods designed for household use. Installment credit in the early 1800s was used in much the same way as it is used today. It was granted specifically for a single purchase and required both a down payment and a formal contract that permitted the merchant to retain title to the article until the purchase price had been paid. For instance, Cowperwaite and Sons, which was founded in New York in 1807 and appears to have been the first firm in the United States to specialize in furniture, sold goods on installment terms from its very inception.

Another type of early credit, which was similar to the revolving credit used by most present-day credit card companies, was known as "open book" credit. While both term and installment credit were used for more expensive items, open book credit was generally used for cheaper goods that were purchased more frequently. Open book credit was most often found in rural areas, but it was also relatively common in many early American cities. Other sources of credit in the early years of the nineteenth century were physicians, who often had to collect their fees on a delayed basis, and pawnbrokers. In New York City, pawnbroking had developed to such an extent that in the year 1828, pawnbrokers reported 149,000 pledges. (A pledge is a consumer loan made with a piece of collateral to secure its repayment.)

As installment credit gradually proved to be successful over the first half of the nineteenth century, manufacturers began to borrow the notion from the merchants. One of the earliest and most successful manufacturers to utilize the installment plan was the Singer Sewing Machine Company. Other manufacturers began to sell big-ticket consumer durables, such as pianos, household organs, and stoves, directly to consumers through agents by about 1850.

The period after the Civil War was characterized by a growing volume of installment credit sales. Following the successful example of Singer and other manufacturers, local merchants, particularly furniture dealers, began to offer installment credit. During the 1870s, installment credit was extended to sales of encyclopedias as well as to sales of all types of household equipment. In the 1880s, some merchants began to sell jewelry on this basis. As foreign immigration accelerated, an increasingly common sight was the "customer peddler" who sold a variety of goods to non-English-speaking arrivals.

A parallel development was the growth of the small loan business, which apparently began in Chicago about 1870 and spread rapidly to other cities throughout the United States. As a result of widespread abuse in this industry, regulation soon arose in many states. Partly to counter the abuses, laws permitting credit unions were passed in 1909. In 1910, Arthur J. Morris opened a bank that made small loans to consumers at a rate of just 6 percent per year. "Morris-plan" loans were made for a variety of purposes but were usually for emergencies and were also most often for relatively small amounts. Over the next decade, Morris plan banks spread to thirty-seven states.

The spurt of industrialization following the Civil War began the long-term trend toward urbanization in the United States. A son who had learned a trade from his father—metalworking, for example—might discover that in another city there was a big demand for his skills and wages were much higher. The gradual movement of family members from rural communities to large cities helped weaken the family bond, as well as the reliance of family members upon one another for the provision of financing.

The increased geographic distance between family members forced many people to depend upon third-party institutions for any financing they might need. They were also encouraged to seek more financing than they had previously used. According to Nugent,

> Incentives to thrift disappeared with intimate community life. Family traditions, conservative consumptive habits, and reputations for stability gave way to competitive standards of living as the principal basis for prestige. These changes helped to explain two important developments in the field of consumer credit which began shortly after the Civil War. One was the extension of installment merchandising to low income classes; the other, the rise of the small loan business.

It is important to note that the vast geographic size of the United States contributed in no small way to the development of its consumer credit industry. In European countries, the much shorter distances that had to be traveled, along with the smaller number of large industrial cities, enabled families to remain not only close but independent of outside institutions in meeting their financial needs. This fact may help explain why the consumer credit industry in general has been far less successful in most European countries than in the United States and why the credit aspect of credit cards may lack some of the appeal to Europeans that it has had to many Americans.

Following the First World War, increasing sales of automobiles, electric washing machines, vacuum cleaners, and other household durables led to strong growth in the use of consumer credit. Merchants, sales finance companies, small loan offices, credit unions, industrial banks, and even some commercial banks expanded their credit operations. In 1928, the First National City Bank of New York, then the largest bank in the world (today's Citibank), organized a personal loan department. According to Harold Cleveland and Thomas Huertas, researchers for Citibank, the bank started making personal loans in response to a plea by the attorney general of New York for more lenders to engage in personal lending to offset the high rates charged by loan sharks. Many other banks followed First National City Bank's lead in spite of their long-standing prejudice against consumer credit.

The importance of the automobile in stimulating and legitimizing consumer credit sales cannot be overemphasized. The growth of installment sales of automobiles tended to remove the stigma that installment selling had acquired at the hands of low-grade installment merchants in the 1890s. All social and economic classes were represented among installment purchasers of automobiles; hence, installment buying acquired respectability. Although some automobile manufacturers, such as Ford, were slow in implementing installment sales plans, other companies embraced this new marketing tool. General Motors soon became the leader in installment sales.

In the period between the First World War and the onset of the Great Depression, open book credit granted by retail merchants also increased. According to data collected by the Department of Commerce, during the first half of 1930 only 47.4 percent of department store sales were made for cash; 7 percent were made on an installment contract basis, and the remaining 45.6 percent were open book. During the Great Depression, which brought a reduction in sales of discretionary items such as durable goods, installment credit decreased significantly while open book credit decreased relatively little, indicating that this type of merchant credit was generally used for cheaper, nondiscretionary items.

The Introduction of the Credit Card

Until about 1930, outstanding consumer credit was dominated by noninstallment credit, largely charge accounts. The growth in the size of retail establishments, as well as in the number of customers and the volume of business, meant that not every charge account customer could be recognized by clerks in the store. Some form of identification became necessary—hence, the credit card.

Prior to World War I, credit cards were issued by a small number of hotels, oil companies, and department stores. They served the dual purpose of identifying a customer with a charge account and providing a mechanism for keeping records of customer purchases. The use of such cards continued to grow after World War I, until the growth was halted by the depression of the 1930s.

Unlike many other types of credit card issuers, the retailers drifted into the credit card industry simply by conducting business as usual. In the United States, a large proportion of retail sales, particularly of discretionary items, had always been made on credit. Thus, the conversion of the retail charge account into a credit card was no more than a change in terminology. Large retailers extended credit to their customers for two reasons. First, credit was necessary to generate many sales, particularly sales of higher priced items such as clothing or consumer durables. Second, a credit account helped bind a customer to a retailer. It is the latter reason that has accounted for the long-lived resistance of many retailers to universal credit cards, which can be used with virtually every retailer.

The use of credit cards by retailers began in 1914 when some large stores gave cards to their wealthier clients. The cards were helpful to store employees in recognizing charge account customers, and regular charge accounts were desirable to the wealthy customers because they could pay for an entire month's purchases at one time, cutting down on their bookkeeping. Used in this fashion, credit cards lent prestige to their owners. However, the credit card's prestige diminished somewhat with the wider distribution of credit cards. By the mid-1930s, two-thirds of Americans using credit cards did so because they did not have cash to pay for their purchases, a vast change from the earlier days.

In 1928, department store credit cards took on a new feature with the introduction of "charga-plates." Produced by the Farrington Manufacturing Company of Boston, these metal plates resembled the Army-issue dog tags and were, in fact, nothing more than reconfigured embossed-address plates. A charge account customer at any of a wide number of department stores would be given such a plate, which, when inserted by the salesperson in a machine known as a recorder, or imprinter, would automatically stamp onto the sales slip the customer's name and address and some coded credit information.

Although retailers regarded the charge account as a means of retaining customer loyalty, they also recognized that shoppers who were not regular customers might be persuaded to buy if they had the necessary credit. Consequently, a number of charge account systems that covered many stores were formed—some covering stores with charge systems of their own. By 1936, the Retail Service Bureau of Seattle had signed up more than 1,000 retail establishments that agreed to honor charges by their joint customers, who received one monthly itemized bill covering all charge purchases. Payments were due on the tenth of the following month. Although the plan included only retailers, it was similar in concept to the Diners Club plan that came along some fifteen years later. By the end of World War II, cooperative credit plans existed in several cities.

While for the retail industry the credit card was simply a natural extension of its existing credit operations, the credit card was a much needed innovation for the oil companies. In marketing their gasoline, the oil companies were faced with a logistical problem not faced by many other retailers of the early twentieth century. Since the automobile was created for traveling, the owner could not be expected to maintain loyalty to one particular service station. Consequently, to keep customers loyal to a particular brand of gasoline, it was necessary to devise a system that would allow a customer to charge fuel purchases at all outlets of a particular company and that, through a consolidation of records, would charge the customer on a monthly basis.

Beginning in the early 1920s, oil companies issued what they called "courtesy" cards, which had all the features of today's gasoline credit cards with two exceptions: they lacked the revolving credit feature, and they were made of paper rather than plastic and were reissued every three to six months. The oil company courtesy cards were issued without charge and did not even need to be applied for since they were given by service station managers to their most frequent customers.

The success of the early courtesy cards prompted other oil companies to issue their own cards. Customers could buy gasoline, oil, and small parts at the service station and were obligated to repay the entire outstanding charge by the end of the month. The plan proved so successful with the favored customers that the oil companies began giving out cards free to virtually every driver they could find. As historian Gerd Weisensee states, "The fact that the card holder owned an automobile was guarantee enough for the oil companies issuing the cards."

As prosperity returned to the United States shortly before the Second World War, oil companies began a major push to expand their cardholder base. In 1939, Standard Oil of Indiana startled the industry with a major campaign to distribute 250,000 new cards in a short period of time. While other companies had more than that number of cards outstanding, they had built their accounts carefully through distribution by local service station managers to trusted customers. Standard Oil of Indiana's mass distribution of cards threatened to establish a new industry norm. According to a 1939 *BusinessWeek* article, "Credit men are nervous lest this new distribution precipitate unforeseen credit woes."

The credit card was a useful marketing tool for the major oil companies, which were trying to sign up individual service station owners. A company boasting several hundred thousand cardholders around the country could hold out the promise of greatly enhanced "drive-in" business from travelers. In addition, by replacing a good customer's existing charge account with a credit card, the dealer could effectively transfer the financing of accounts receivable to the oil company, since the charge ticket was accepted by the oil company as cash in paying for gasoline delivery.

However, as the credit card industry would learn again and again until the practice was outlawed by Congress in 1970, the mass distribution of unsolicited credit cards was detrimental as well as beneficial. The benefit was the quick establishment of a large cardholder base that held merchants in place and gained market share. The cost, however, came quickly in the form of large initial losses due to fraud. A 25 November 1939 *BusinessWeek* article, "Oil Men Jumpy over Credit Cards," reported that

> a credit card gone wrong is the next thing to a book of signed blank checks or an unlimited letter of credit. One cardholder went haywire and began earning his living by carrying passengers between New York and California for less than bus fare. The gas and oil bill for his transcontinental taxicab passed $500 before he committed an unrelated federal offense and landed in jail. (38–39)

In those days, as now, credit cards were substantial money-losers for the oil companies. According to a 1939 survey carried out by the oilmen's section of the National Association of Credit Men and reported in the 1 November 1939 edition of *National Petroleum News*, the total cost of the credit card business over cash business averaged 0.85¢ per gallon, or 4.85 percent of the sale. And then, as now, problems of credit card fraud abounded. Dealers often sold unauthorized merchandise or services to cardholders, or even advanced money to cardholders while making out a slip only for gasoline. The practice of overcharging the customer became so widespread that, as the survey reported, companies were forced to "scrutinize all large tickets microscopically, threaten to revoke a dealer's charge privilege when they catch him charging 17 gallons into a 14 gallon tank or selling 40 gallons in one day to the owner of one Chevrolet."

One of the last major industries to introduce credit cards was the airline industry. Airline travel cards dated back to 1931 when Century Airlines began offering coupon books for airplane trips at a discount of 15 percent off list price. The use of these prepaid coupons enabled travelers to fly without having to carry large amounts of cash. After it acquired Century Airlines, American Airlines also adopted this service.

Charles R. Speers, a Detroit traffic manager for American, helped make coupon books more appealing to corporate customers by having the coupons on file with the airline, thereby enabling any of each customer's employees to fly on those coupons. Speer proposed a modified system to the General Motors Pontiac Division, his largest commercial account, whereby American would hold two of Pontiac's $250 coupon books on file in its Detroit office. When an employee flew American, Pontiac would supply an authorization letter permitting the airline to remove the necessary coupons. When the value of the coupons dropped to $250, another book would be purchased. In 1936, the coupon books were replaced by a deposit of $425, which was the equivalent of two $250 coupon books minus a discount. (American Airlines later renamed its program the Universal Air Travel Plan [UATP] and allowed other airlines to join.)

As the country moved into the 1940s, it finally seemed ready to push out of the economic doldrums of the 1930s. The credit card industry in particular—as indicated by Standard Oil of Indiana's ambitious if unsuccessful mass mailing effort and the variety of new credit plans being implemented in various other industries—seemed poised to take advantage of the economic recovery. Those plans were put on the back burner, however, with the onset of the Second World War. Wartime credit restrictions and the slowdown in consumer spending forced most firms to put their credit card operations on hold. Gas was rationed, temporarily closing down the oil companies' credit card operations, and the use of installment credit to finance purchases was greatly diminished by regulations placed on it by the Federal Reserve, which set minimum down payments and maximum repayment periods for the purchase of large consumer durables.

As World War II ended, however, the United States stood poised for a major economic expansion. Prosperity, always just around the corner during the 1930s, had finally arrived, with much fanfare. After four years of churning out fighter planes, warships, tanks, and rifles, the country was ready to turn its newly developed economic muscle to the more peaceful and more profitable production of automobiles, homes, dishwashers, and clothing.

3

Universal Cards: The Early Years

BOTH ECONOMICALLY AND PSYCHOLOGI-cally, postwar America was primed to take advantage of the onslaught of consumer goods. Victories in Europe and the South Pacific had raised confidence in the country to a new high. The Social Security system, now firmly entrenched, promised every American a secure old age. Other government programs, such as worker's compensation and unemployment and disability insurance, and the spread of life insurance contributed to a growing sense of economic security for millions of Americans. But most importantly, for the first time in the century the average American family's income exceeded the cost of its basic needs. Discretionary income, a term previously unknown to most Americans, became the watchword of this new era of growth in consumer credit.

Consumer credit grew at a phenomenal rate in the twenty-five years following World War II. In 1945, consumer credit stood at $5.7 billion. By 1970, it had grown to $143.1 billion, and by 1980 to over $375 billion, excluding mortgage debt.

With the stage appropriately set, companies prepared to revive their dormant credit operations. The oil companies, retailers, and airlines all moved back into the credit card field. They brought with them a number of new programs and technological innovations as they sought new ways to expand their operations and achieve the profits that had eluded them earlier.

Just prior to the Second World War, Mobil, Gulf, and Standard Oil together had more than one million cards in existence. Because of the rationing of gas during the war, all of those cardholders had been lost. At war's end, in an attempt to rebuild their cardholder base, several large oil companies sent free cards to their prewar customers. They also began marketing campaigns to new college graduates, who received either an unsolicited card or an application for a card. In spite of the high cost of the card program and the misgivings of many oil companies, competitive pressures forced all oil companies to follow suit. Many of the companies also began to allow their customers to repay purchases in monthly installments, a practice that had seen limited use prior to the war.

A major innovation for the gasoline credit cards during this period was the introduction in 1952 of a metal credit card. Although metal charga-plates had been used by department stores since 1928, the oil companies had clung to the paper charge cards they had always issued. The new metal charge card was developed by the Standard Oil Company of California, which called it the Chevromatic, to link it to its Chevron-brand gasoline. The system was ordered from the Farrington Manufacturing Company, which had long supplied charga-plates to the department stores.

While other oil companies had in fact experimented with the idea before, they had given it up as being too expensive. Standard decided to fully implement the procedure in 1952 following a twelve-month pilot project in Arizona. That project revealed that the use of such standardized plates cut errors in identification by 94 percent. In addition, chargebacks to dealers due to being unable to identify purchasers were cut by 80 percent, and the time spent in making out sales slips by 50 percent. To keep the familiar appearance of the paper credit card, Standard clamped the embossed aluminum plate onto the back of the card, thereby creating the embossed, full-size credit card that would later be made from plastic. These cards were distributed to all of Standard's half a million customers in the western United States.

The Origins of Revolving Credit

Retailers also reentered the credit card industry with a number of new innovations. By far the most important of these was the refinement of the concept of revolving credit. As we have seen, retailers offered credit in various forms to their customers to stimulate sales of goods and retain customer loyalty. As in other industries, retailers considered credit to be a costly but necessary expense of doing business. Presumably, the cost of the credit operation could be buried in the prices charged for the merchandise.

As department store chains expanded and began to pursue less affluent segments of the population, they were faced with a new problem: How could credit be offered to this new market? Open book credit within a charge account system was not considered feasible because the higher expected collection costs and lower expected average transaction would make such an arrangement unprofitable.

The first step toward revolving credit was taken in the late 1930s by Wanamaker's of Philadelphia, which allowed customers to repay charge accounts in four monthly payments without interest. The first store to actually use the revolving credit system—or "rotating charge account," as it was called at that time—appears to have been the L. Bamberger & Company department store of Newark, New Jersey. Bamberger's rotating charge account was begun by William B. Gorman, who would introduce it in 1947 at Gimbel Bros. of New York.

With this plan, the customer was given a fixed credit line for the purchase of soft goods such as clothing. Big-ticket items could be financed, as always, through the regular installment plan. Each month the customer was required to repay one-sixth of the balance plus an interest charge of one percent on the unpaid balance. Gorman set a six-month limit because he believed that it was "psychologically unsound" for a customer to keep paying for merchandise after it had worn out. Following Gorman's introduction of the rotating charge at Gimbel's in 1947, *BusinessWeek* (8 March 1947) summarized the advantages of the plan:

> For Gimbels, which caters to customers with low or moderate incomes, the plan is peculiarly suitable. It permits extension of credit to those who otherwise could not qualify. For example, a $50-a-week salary might be the minimum for granting a regular charge account, but a rotating account can be offered to a customer earning as little as $25 a week, if other factors are favorable. Such customers are unlikely to have more than one charge account, even of the limited variety, which helps assure their loyalty to Gimbels.
>
> The rotating plan also enables the store to extend credit to another consistent buyer who would be a poor risk otherwise— the "career girl" who earns a modest salary and spends most of it on clothes. The plan is probably more advantageous to stores in metropolitan areas, where the population is relatively transient, than to those in smaller, more stable communities. Gimbels will plug it as a means of tiding families over buying peaks like Christmas and Easter.

The original revolving charge plan had been adopted by a number of stores, including Filene's of Boston and Bloomingdale's of New York, before it filtered down to Gimbel's after the Second World War. However, it was not until several years later, in 1956, that J. L. Hudson's in Detroit added the last innovation to the credit system we know today—the interest-free period. Under Hudson's plan, customers could either repay the balance within thirty days without a finance charge or as little as one-quarter of the outstanding balance each month with a finance charge. It should be noted that with this final innovation, the department stores could combine their three types of credit programs—the regular charge account for preferred customers, the revolving charge account for customers who preferred to pay over time, and the installment account. In so doing, stores were eventually able to realize cost savings in handling their credit transactions.

Following the war, a number of large retailers joined together to form cooperative card operations similar to those begun in the 1930s. In 1948, a number of major New York department stores, including Bloomingdale's, Arnold Constable, Franklin Simon, Gimbel's, and Saks, began a charga-plate group; the standard charga-plates they mailed to their customers were usable at any of the cooperating stores. The system offered several advantages, the primary one being that persons who had charge accounts at several stores did not have to carry a large number of heavy metal plates.

Since not all customers had accounts at all the stores in a charga-plate group, it was a common practice to notch the cards so that they would fit only the imprinters of stores with which a customer had an account. The central agency that handled distribution of the plates also handled servicing and changes of address. In addition, the agency served as a type of credit bureau: stores investigating a new customer's credit application could see whether the applicant had charge accounts in other charga-plate stores.

Development of the Universal Cards

In many ways, the cooperative credit card operation was quite similar to the universal credit card operations that would soon follow. However, there were two important differences. First, although each retailer's card could be used at a limited number of stores, each retailer also retained its identity and relationship with its customers. Second, cooperative credit cards still served only as a means of facilitating a well-established function—the extension of credit to customers as an aid to selling products, not as a profit-making operation. One last major conceptual step remained to be taken: a true "universal" credit card would be one that was tied to neither a single vendor nor a single product, and that not only allowed the user to purchase goods in many places but allowed the issuer to make a profit.

Initially, there were two types of universal credit cards (although the distinctions between them have dulled in recent years): the travel and entertainment cards that were issued by American Express, Diners Club and Carte Blanche, and the bank cards, issued by BankAmericard and MasterCharge. Although the T&E cards were developed first, they were overtaken by the much more numerous bank cards, which duplicated their services and for which comparable annual fees were ultimately charged.

The first universal card plan, though quite limited in scope, was developed by John C. Biggins, an innovative banker and consumer credit specialist at the Flatbush National Bank of Brooklyn, New York. In 1947, Biggins initiated a local community credit plan, which he called Charg-It, for a two-square-block neighborhood in the vicinity of the bank. Biggins's plan was relatively successful and was later adopted by the Paterson Savings and Trust Company of Paterson, New Jersey, in 1950. His plan had much greater significance, however, for the credit industry because it ushered in the era of the third-party, universal credit card—without a doubt, the most important development in the history of credit cards.

Although Biggins was the first to develop a true universal credit card, Diners Club, as we have already seen, was the first to implement and market such a card successfully on a large scale. Only a year after its formation in 1949, Diners Club had managed to sign up 285 establishments and 35,000 cardholders, who were each charged $3 per year for their cards. At the end of the following year, 1951, Diners Club was in the black, showing a profit of $61,222 on total sales of $6.2 million.

The quick success of Diners Club caused it to expand rapidly, not only geographically but also in services. The company pushed to sign up merchants in such industries as hotels, airlines, gas stations, retail stores, and automobile rental companies. In the mid-1950s, Diners Club expanded into Europe through franchise agreements. This period was marked, however, by strong resistance from merchants to the plan. The Diners Club card, and later, the other universal cards, was resisted for two reasons: many companies did not wish to pay the discount, and the existence of a credit card that could be used at all types of establishments substantially weakened the retailer's relationship with its customers.

Leading the opposition to the T&E cards were European and U.S.

hotel trade associations, which prohibited their members from accepting credit cards that had discounts, effectively ruling out the T&E cards. In England and Switzerland, members who accepted such cards were thrown out of their hotel trade associations. As a result, the British and Swedish hotel and restaurant associations left the international association and created their own association. In so doing, they established the BHR credit card, which later became the EuroCard. Initially, EuroCard attempted to operate without a merchant discount, charging only the cardholder. That practice resulted in significant losses, and consequently, EuroCard was forced to add a discount for restaurants and hotels. The European hotel associations held out the longest in their opposition to the T&E cards. Eventually the competition and market pressures forced them to drop their boycotts of the cards, and they agreed to pay discounts of up to 5 percent.

Following a similar course, the American Hotel Association introduced its own credit card, the Universal Travel Card, which did not have a discount for the hotels. The plan was neither successful nor inexpensive, and in 1958 the Universal Travel Card was taken over by American Express, which thus gained about 4,500 merchants and 160,000 cardholders.

In 1957, the oil companies, then embroiled in a major marketing war, entered into an industrywide interchange agreement in an attempt to block out all third-party universal cards. All of the major oil companies except Texaco agreed to honor the cards of each other through the exchange network. The oil companies resisted outside credit cards primarily because of the discount that they were forced to pay.

It should be noted that the boycott of universal cards by the oil companies was only a last-ditch effort after their own attempts at developing a universal gas card had failed. In 1949, the Frontier Refining Company of Denver gave its dealers permission to accept sales made on "foreign" credit cards, provided that a 6 percent service charge was made. And in 1951, National Credit Card, Inc., an independent credit agency, initiated a universal credit card for the oil companies with a $20 membership fee for dealers and a 6 percent service charge for dealers.

Aside from the smaller oil companies, which did not operate their own credit card plans, there was not much acceptance of this independent universal credit card. According to the 19 November 1952 issue of *National Petroleum News*, the obstacles to a universally accepted credit card in the early 1950s included the cost of accepting such cards (reckoned at 2.5¢ per gallon), the lack of understanding by members of the general public, who would not like the idea of being billed by a "strange" company, and the small amount of business that most stations could hope to attract in largely pre-expressway America. With the failure of National Credit Card in 1954, the universal credit card did not exist in the oil industry until the interchange agreement three years later.

Another major obstacle to the T&E card was the boycott by the International Air Transport Association (IATA). Like the hotel organization, the IATA had its own travel card, the Universal Air Travel Plan (UATP). By 1958, UATP was maintaining regular deposits of $425 from each of its over 800,000 cardholders. It had no interest in allowing the T&E cards to enter into competition with it for this lucrative market. The refusal of the airlines, particularly the international airlines, to accept the T&E cards did not really end until 1964, when the prohibition was lifted with the help of the U.S. Civil Aeronautics Board (CAB).

Competition

As difficult as it was for Diners Club to overcome all of these obstacles, its most serious challenge would come from competitors within the credit card field. Throughout most of the 1950s, it had the field almost entirely to itself, with the exception of a number of smaller bank credit card operations. In 1958, Diners Club's position changed dramatically with the advent of two formidable competitors, American Express and Carte Blanche.

American Express had decided to enter the credit card business mostly as a hedge against possible inroads the industry might make into the lucrative traveler's check business. The traveler's check had been invented in 1890 by Marcellus Fleming Barry, an employee of the American Express Company. Barry had developed the traveler's check in response to a challenge from the head of American Express, J. C. Fargo, to solve the problem of cashing personal checks while abroad. Barry's innovation of putting a line at the top of a check to be signed at the time of purchase and a line at the bottom for the comparison signature when the check was cashed was copyrighted in 1891 and has survived relatively unchanged to this day.

Survival, however, was very much a concern at American Express when, after studying the credit card business for several years, it issued its first credit card on 1 October 1958. Its first year of operation ended with some 32,000 establishments accepting the cards and more than 475,000 cardholders signed up. In large part, its initial success was due to its takeover of the Universal Travel Card issued by the American Hotel Association. However, by the early 1960s, the growing dominance of American Express in the T&E field was more directly related to its existing international connections through its traveler's check operations and, perhaps more importantly, the enormous financial resources that it could draw upon to support its marketing and financial operations. These resources far surpassed those of either of its two rivals.

Carte Blanche, the second major entrant into the T&E credit card field, was originally the private credit card of the Hilton Hotel Corporation. Founded as a separate entity in 1958, it was sold in 1965 to the FNCB Services Corporation, a subsidiary of the First National City Bank of New York (later Citibank). In response to a suit filed by the antitrust division of the Justice Department, the First National City Bank agreed to run Carte Blanche as an independent corporation. In April 1968, control of Carte Blanche was sold to the Avco Corporation, which bought 51 percent of the outstanding shares from First National City Bank. In December 1969, the remaining shares were purchased from the Hilton Hotels.

Following the limited efforts by the Flatbush National Bank and the Paterson Savings and Trust Company to establish community credit plans, a number of other banks, such as the Franklin National Bank of New York, entered the credit card field on a limited basis. By 1955, there were more than 100 banks with credit card plans. Most were smaller operations, however, because most larger banks were still reluctant to enter into this as yet unproven field.

At the beginning of the 1950s, the majority of banks did not promote consumer credit of any kind. If a bank had a consumer loan department, it was often found in the basement where no one could see the furtive borrower. Gradually, it became clear to the banks that, in contrast to their commercial loan customers, consumers were not as sensitive to interest rates. That difference meant that profit margins on consumer loans could be potentially much higher than on commercial loans. But it was not until the banking heavyweights, Bank of America and Chase Manhattan Bank, the country's largest and second-largest banks, launched credit card operations that the banking industry entered the credit card field in earnest.

Initially, the bank cards operated much like the T&E cards except that bank cards required no annual fee. Consequently, since credit was extended on a thirty-day basis with no charge, the only revenue for the banks came from the discounts obtained from the participating merchants. The banks soon found, however, that these discounts were not sufficient to pay the operating costs of the cards. In 1958 and 1959, following the lead of the retailers, many banks introduced a new credit card plan that featured the option of repaying balances on a revolving credit basis. Aside from its attraction to cardholders, revenue from the monthly interest charge on balances usually made the difference between the profitability and nonprofitability of bank credit card plans.

The growth of bank credit card plans was slowed somewhat by startup and operational difficulties. A prime example was the Chase Manhattan Charge Plan (CMCP). Introduced in 1958 at about the same time BankAmericard was opening its operations on the West Coast, CMCP had 350,000 cardholders and 5,300 retail merchants by the end of its first year of operation. Cardholders were sent a single monthly bill. They were given a ten-day grace period to settle their bill, after which they were charged one percent of the unpaid balance. Credit could be extended for up to five months. Merchants were charged a 6 percent discount, with refunds on volume that could reduce this figure to as low as 2 percent.

By 1960, CMCP sales volume had grown to $25 million. However, the number of cardholders had fallen to 160,000, and as credit losses and operating expenses mounted, the entire operation fell back into the red. In January 1962, Chase Manhattan gave up and sold CMCP to Uni-Serve for $9 million. Uni-Serve was a new corporation that had been formed expressly for this purpose by Joseph P. Williams, who had gained experience in the credit card industry on the West Coast. Uni-Serve began to market the card under the new name of Uni-Card.

The demise of CMCP, coupled with the many operational difficulties experienced by the Bank of America, caused other banks to proceed very slowly. The general feeling at this early stage seemed to be that if the two largest banks in the country experienced problems and high expenses with their credit card operations, it was doubtful that smaller banks would be able to operate them profitably.

While other banks continued to have difficulties, Bank of America, in spite of its own operational difficulties, continued to grow rapidly. A major advantage was its large branch network throughout California, which gave it quick access to a large and affluent customer base. Because most bank card plans between 1959 and 1966 operated independently of each other, a large network was crucial to developing a sufficiently large cardholder and merchant base. Another key to its success was more apparent than real, as John David Wilson has noted in his 1986 book, *The Chase.* Unlike Chase Manhattan, which fully charged all expenses to its credit card operation, Bank of America chose not to charge the cost of funds or advertising to its credit card operation. That practice allowed its credit card operation to appear profitable, while Chase's more realistic accounting procedures showed its credit card operating at a loss.

In 1966, Bank of America announced that it would license the operation of its BankAmericard across the United States. To compete with this formidable organization, several other large banks formed a second national card system, known as the Interbank Card Association.

The idea behind the national interchanges set up by BankAmericard and Interbank was to enable the cardholder to use a credit card for purchasing goods in areas served by other banks. Such an arrangement made it possible to transfer sales drafts from the bank of the merchant who accepted payment with the credit card to the bank of the cardholder for collection. Since merchants and cardholders were tied to local banks, a method was needed to transfer credits among banks if a cardholder served by one bank made a credit card purchase from a merchant served by another bank. The interchange, in effect, transformed local cards into national cards. By so doing, the cards became more useful to customers. In addition, since the size of the market became larger for merchants, the card also became more attractive to them. Formation of the interchanges also put pressure on banks that were not already members to sign up in order to keep or generate business from the cardholding consumer, as well as from merchant depositors.

Some three years after its formation, Interbank did not have a satisfactory identification device similar to BankAmericard's. Consequently, in 1969 it purchased the rights to "Master Charge" from the Western States Bank Card Association, and most Interbank members changed over to the Master Charge card. A year later, in 1970, as a result of pressure from BankAmericard franchise holders, the BankAmericard operation was spun off from Bank of America and placed under the control of the newly formed organization National BankAmericard, Inc. (NBI). NBI's role was to unite member bank credit card operations and achieve a more uniform marketing plan. To do so, it was necessary to institute and enforce stringent operating regulations, which were backed by stiff fines. Eventually the Bank of America relinquished its central role in the bank interchange organization. As a result, the NBI and Interbank organizations became somewhat similar in structure, and both are now completely independent entities.

The close of the 1960s marked the end of the first major period of expansion for the universal credit card industry. Through much effort, the groundwork had been laid for a period of major growth. National and international credit networks were in place, and the process of consolidation had begun. The earlier distinctions between the T&E and bank cards had been largely erased, and both now operated in fairly similar fashion. The banks had also overtaken the T&E companies in number of cards issued and held a secure lead in that area. The one major remaining distinction was the annual fee imposed by the T&E cards.

In the T&E field, Carte Blanche, Diners Club, and, in particular, American Express dominated the industry. Among bank cards, the two competing interchanges—Interbank and NBI—were clearly the leaders. What was needed was a mechanism to generate the large cardholder base needed to move to the next level of growth.

4

Bank Cards: The Growth Years

By THE LATE 1960s, THE BANK CREDIT CARD industry had more or less stabilized. The once numerous and isolated bank card plans had given way, with a few exceptions, to two dominant national organizations—BankAmericard and Master Charge. Features such as the discount rate and revolving credit had become more or less standardized, and other operational problems, such as processing, while still daunting, had been eased somewhat by the beneficial effect of increased economies of scale. The primary problem now facing the banks was how to develop a large cardholder base. The strategy they chose was neither new nor by anyone's account problem-free. However, it had one compelling attribute to recommend it—it worked.

Mailings of Unsolicited Cards

As we have seen in previous chapters, mass mailings of unsolicited credit cards had been tried nearly thirty years before by Standard Oil of Indiana with its gasoline credit card. Eventually the strategy was discredited: the oil companies discovered that while such mailings did significantly expand their cardholder base, they also led to a huge increase in losses due to fraud. When the bank card companies decided to try the same strategy, they were aware of the history and the drawbacks of mass mailings, and they fully expected to incur considerable losses.

However, the bank card companies also knew that they had to generate a significant amount of revenue to offset the high startup costs of their programs. Furthermore, the fragmented structure of the bank card industry, which was made up of thousands of card-issuing banks, made mass mailings the only workable solution.

In preparing their campaigns, both BankAmericard and Master Charge worked feverishly to beat the other to the punch. They realized that most people would not be able to differentiate between a BankAmericard and a Master Charge card. Therefore, the one that could mail its cards more quickly to more people would gain the largest cardholder base.

As expected, not long after they had instituted the unsolicited credit card programs in the late 1960s, the banks began to experience significant losses due to fraud. In 1964, the U.S. Post Office investigated only fifteen cases of credit card fraud. In 1968, that figure shot up to 360, and the following year it more than doubled to 762. Figures compiled in 1970 by Andrew Brimmer, one of the Federal Reserve Board's seven governors, showed that bank charge card losses had increased 50 percent that year to $115.5 million, or 3.4 percent of the $3.4 billion in outstanding credit card debt—compared with $20 million just four years earlier.

In large part, these losses were caused by placing credit cards in the hands of people who were bad credit risks, an inevitable development when customers were not screened, and by the theft of thousands of cards by individuals who were quick to identify the vulnerability of the system. Not only did losses for the banks mount, but there were also loud complaints from innocent customers who received no card and large bills. Although the banks soon developed appropriate safeguards against thefts, their initial reluctance to protect customers led the Federal Trade Commission (FTC) to ban mailings of unsolicited credit cards in May 1970.

Despite these initial problems, the mailings did achieve their primary goal—the rapid establishment of large cardholder bases. As far as the banks were concerned, this achievement alone was well worth all of the losses and aggravation. With new bases to draw upon, the industry could now embark on a major expansion. During the 1970s, the number of bank credit cards in circulation would more than double and charge volume would increase by 1400 percent as the bank card industry matured into a worldwide industry.

Bank card operations experienced record growth in 1970. Interbank merchant outlets increased by 24 percent over the previous year. The total number of accounts rose by 9 percent, and the dollar volume of sales reached nearly $3.5 billion. BankAmericard reported similar growth, with sales in 1970 up 57 percent over the previous year. The number of merchants accepting BankAmericard was up 31 percent, and the total number of cards in circulation had reached 26 million. Although the 1970 ban on unsolicited cards led to a moderate but temporary drop in the banks' cardholder base, charge volumes continued to increase, as did the number of banks and merchant outlets participating in the credit card interchanges. As a side benefit, the ban on unsolicited cards also reduced the amount of charge-offs on unpaid and fraudulent accounts.

In retrospect, the ban on unsolicited cards probably came at an opportune time for the bank card companies. They needed time to adjust their operations to handle the huge increase in cardholders and to make these newly acquired accounts profitable. Despite their rapid growth, bank cards still represented only 11 percent of all credit cards in use in 1973. (Retail store cards accounted for 54 percent, oil company cards for 27 percent, T&E cards for 2 percent, and 6 percent were all others.) The increasing rate of inflation that began in 1973 with the Arab oil embargo contributed to an upsurge in credit card use, but the rising cost of money reduced the profit potential of the banks. As notes on routine commercial loans climbed to 12 percent and higher, and legal ceilings on consumer loans held in the 20 percent range, the differential was temporarily not great enough to justify further expansion in cardholder bases.

The short lull, therefore, seemed to energize the industry. In 1974, many bank credit card operations experienced their best year ever as both BankAmericard and Master Charge posted new highs in numbers of cardholders, finally surpassing their pre-ban levels. Sales volume and cash advances were also up 25 and 30 percent, respectively. Even the banks' decision to increase the discount charged to merchants in response to the rise in interest rates could not slow the industry's growth.

That move, made in the summer of 1974, upset the small businesses that formed the bulk of participating merchants. In fact, a poll taken in November 1974 by the National Federation of Independent Business projected a downturn in the proportion of retail stores honoring bank cards. But instead of dropping, as most analysts predicted, the number of outlets accepting the cards increased substantially. The rising sales volume had "hooked" the merchants who were unable to forgo the card-oriented portion of their business, even in the face of higher discounts.

Marketing efforts during this period were much more conservative; companies were seeking to avoid the losses they had incurred through the mass mailings. Most banks concentrated their marketing efforts on upper-middle–income Americans, assuming that this group would be the most creditworthy. Unfortunately, while it was indeed more creditworthy than lower income groups, its members also tended to repay their billings on time, a habit that cost the bank card industry much of its interest income. Since interest income accounted for nearly two-thirds of total operating income, banks were forced to gear their marketing efforts toward a lower income market and accept somewhat higher charge-offs if they were to improve overall profitability.

In 1970, Master Charge and BankAmericard began to market plans to give free cards to virtually any college student. One such plan gave a card to any student who was registered for at least three credits, regardless of age, background, credit rating, or bank balance. The motive was to build lifetime loyalty to a card by getting it into the hands of a businessperson or professional at the start of his or her career. Both Diners Club and American Express had experimented with giving credit cards to college students in the 1960s and had found that their losses were quite high. Banks soon learned that same lesson on their own. As subsequent events would prove, only a fraction of college students were mature enough to be entrusted with a substantial line of credit.

While promotion to college students was enthusiastically pursued, a few industry professionals began to question its basic premise, the establishment of brand loyalty. Some felt that the plan could rebound if the cards encouraged students to get into debt difficulties. Negative early experiences might influence their attitudes toward credit cards for the rest of their lives.

A few student bank card marketing plans were successful. Wells Fargo Bank, for example, tested the potential of its bank card in the college student market with a mailing to 5,000 graduate students at Stanford University in 1970. The mailing resulted in a 20 percent return, and the accounts tended to be used immediately, with balances averaging $150 (over a five-month span), and were almost never delinquent. However, the elite population chosen for that test could hardly be emulated on a widespread basis.

Some of those who defended the student marketing program justified the inferior payment record on the grounds that the issuers were not set up to handle students who were on campus only nine months of the year. Bills forwarded during the summer were received late and paid late. The solution would have been a new billing procedure tailored to the special needs of the college student. Despite their unsuccessful experience with them, credit card companies continue to mount college student marketing campaigns every few years to meet marketing goals, always with the same lackluster results.

Although the mid-1970s was a period of rapid growth for both BankAmericard and Master Charge, not all banks abandoned their own credit cards. In fact, many proponents of electronic funds transfer (EFT) predicted that banks would move back to a bank's own unique card to retain their identity. As we will see, banks did not leave the two major credit card companies.

Preston State Bank of Dallas, one of the very earliest credit card issuers in the United States, revived its Presto Charge card. Largely confined to local North Dallas merchants, Presto Charge was revived ostensibly to help serve first-time credit card applicants. Designed by William R. Buckley, president of Preston Bank, it provided customers who would normally be turned down with a means of both establishing and proving their ability to manage credit.

Target markets included students, people in their twenties, and persons who were recently divorced. Prior to reviving its Presto Charge card, Preston State Bank had 270,000 Master Charge cards outstanding. Buckley calculated that 54 percent of all Master Charge applications had been turned down, and that 83 percent of these were denied because they lacked credit history. His bank, which was the sixth-largest in Dallas, was located in the wealthiest section of that booming city, and he felt that first-time cardholders from affluent families would prove to be profitable bank customers over the long run. Although Preston Bank's farsighted policy did not attract much emulation at the time, it was a definite forerunner of the movement to private cards in the 1980s.

Consolidation: The BankAmericard– Master Charge Race

The rapid expansion of bank cards both in the United States and abroad, and the ensuing fierce competition for cardholders, led to a growing concentration of power within the industry. By the late 1970s, fifty banks were issuing over half of all bank cards in the United States. Not surprisingly, the largest bank card issuer was Bank of America, with more than 6.7 million cards in circulation and an annual volume of $3.7 billion. It was followed, in order, by Citibank, with 5.6 million cards in circulation and an annual volume of $2.2 billion, First National of Chicago, with more than 3 million cardholders, Chase Manhattan Bank with 2.9 million cardholders, and Continental of Chicago with 2.2 million cardholders.

The move toward concentration had gained considerable momentum in 1978 when, following two years of continued strong growth in the industry, several large banks began to market their cards aggressively, first outside their own market areas and then across the entire country. The initial incursions into rival banks' territory were often followed by attempts to acquire entire credit card operations from those banks, which were unable to compete effectively, were tired of absorbing losses from credit cards, or needed cash for other reasons.

One of the first to begin expanding its credit card operations throughout the country was Continental Bank of Chicago. Using prospect names prescreened through credit bureaus, Continental pursued new credit card customers wherever the combination of demographics and response to prior tests yielded cardholders on a cost-effective basis. Although no figures were released by Continental, its mailings were believed to total nearly three million, with a return ranging from 10 to 20 percent. To minimize complaints from its correspondent banks, Continental gave advance notice of all mailings in a correspondent's area.

The generally low-key approach of Continental was in sharp contrast to the far more aggressive policy of Citibank, the nation's second-largest bank. Citibank saw the credit card as its key to building a nationwide retail market in advance of anticipated legislation making full-scale interstate branching a possibility. It was not at all reticent about moving into direct competition with other banks in its pursuit of new customers. For example, as part of its marketing strategy, Citibank often attempted to lure cardholders away from their present banks by offering a significantly higher line of credit.

As Citibank expanded its nationwide marketing, it also began to look for a new home. Relatively low usury ceilings in New York State restricted profits and made the possibility of moving its credit card business to another state very attractive. Eventually Citibank's credit card operation did leave New York for the unlikely location of South Dakota, where labor was cheaper, rents were lower, and regulations were less restrictive.

Although the strength of individual banks would grow throughout the 1970s, the bank card industry continued to be dominated by the two companies that the banks had formed to help facilitate their entry into the credit card industry—BankAmericard and Master Charge. By 1978, more than 11,000 U.S. banks were associated with either one or both of these card companies. Most banks could not issue BankAmericard and Master Charge cards themselves. Rather, they were agent or affiliate banks: they offered credit card services to merchant customers and accepted sales slips for deposits but did not themselves carry the outstanding credit. The agent banks were thus freed from many of the risks of running a credit card operation, but they were also excluded from participation in the profits accruing to revolving card balances. Some card-issuing banks made private arrangements with smaller banks to provide central accounting and billing services and even issue cards in the name of the smaller bank.

National BankAmericard, Inc. had been incorporated in July 1970 with headquarters in San Francisco. The initial officers were Samuel B. Stewart, chairman of the board, who was also vice chairman of the board of Bank of America, and Dee W. Hock, president, who was then vice president of National Bank of Commerce, Seattle. Set up as a Delaware corporation without capital stock, NBI was made up of 246 Class A large banks and 3,505 Class B smaller banks. The functions of Class A banks were to issue cards to customers, extend credit to and collect payment from cardholders, interchange drafts, and provide authorization services. Class B banks acted as sales agents for the Class A banks. In exchange for distributing the Class A bank's cards to their customers, Class B banks were allowed to put their names on the cards and often received a portion of the fee income, without the considerable investment needed to become a Class A bank. Under this agreement, the sponsoring Class A member provided many of the necessary administrative services such as handling interchange drafts. The initial consumer marketing theme of BankAmericard was "Think of it as money."

In 1971, BankAmericard announced that it would set up an independent national authorization system to further enhance the effectiveness of its credit card operations. During the early years of the NBI partnership, many banks continued to fear the possible domination of BankAmericard by the powerful Bank of America. As the largest bank in the country, Bank of America was a rival of many banks across the country for nonconsumer business such as commercial loans; within California, it also competed for consumer business. In fact, all non-California banks suspected that they would also eventually find themselves in competition for consumer business with Bank of America when interstate banking became a reality.

Banks that were considering joining BankAmericard were fearful that domination of the cooperative by a rival could lead to potential conflicts of interest in other areas. These fears were heightened somewhat when NBI selected Bank of America's advertising agency as its own. In addition, NBI and Bank of America shared the same law firm, and NBI offices were located in Bank of America's World Headquarters Building in San Francisco. NBI's president, Dee Hock, consistently denied charges of undue influence by Bank of America, but it took several years for these fears to diminish significantly.

At the beginning of the 1970s, Interbank/Master Charge held a sizable lead over NBI, with nearly a 40 percent edge in both sales and cardholders. Denied the only proven mechanism for achieving rapid growth—the mass mailings—and now operating in a much more mature marketplace, NBI seemed unlikely to overtake its rival.

But NBI unexpectedly gained considerable ground when it announced, on 19 January 1972, that it had acquired Uni-Card from Chase Manhattan Bank. Begun by Chase in 1958, the CMCP (Chase Manhattan Charge Plan) card had incurred substantial losses before being sold to Uni-Serve in 1962 for $9 million. Renamed Uni-Card, it subsequently became a division of American Express before being repurchased in early 1969 by Chase for about $50 million. The second time around proved no more profitable than the first; Chase estimated its annual losses at $3 million.

The prime motive for the association of Uni-Card and BankAmericard was the latter's need for a strong outlet in New York City. Banker's Trust was distributing BankAmericards in New York but was not aggressive enough to suit NBI management. NBI's pressing need for a stronger New York affiliate enabled Chase to drive a hard bargain. However, Chase's request to call the new card Uni-Card-BankAmericard was turned down by Dee Hock because he did not want to lose his company's identity. At the time of its sale to NBI, Uni-Card had approximately two million credit cards outstanding.

Duality and Antitrust

The competition between NBI and Interbank came to a head in the mid-1970s over the issue of duality. Duality referred to the issuance of both major bank cards by a single bank. The concept of duality went back several years. Prior to 1971, banks that issued credit cards were associated with either BankAmericard or Master Charge. This clear division would be breached by Worthen Bank and Trust Company of Little Rock, Arkansas. Prior to gaining approval as a full member of Interbank in April 1971, Worthen had been a charter member of NBI. It was a Class A bank with over 59,000 BankAmericards outstanding, contracts with 1,470 merchants, and agency agreements with fifty-eight Class B banks, which in turn had contracts with an additional 2,332 merchants.

Following its acceptance as a member of Interbank, Worthen signed a license agreement to issue Master Charge cards in July 1971. Shortly thereafter, on 14 October, NBI passed an amendment to its bylaws, Bylaw 216, to block dual bank card operations by any of its members. As a result of this ruling, Worthen filed suit in U.S. District Court under Sections 4 and 16 of the Clayton Act seeking declaratory judgment that NBI's new bylaw amendment violated the Sherman Antitrust Act. It asked for treble damages, which were unspecified at that time.

NBI pushed ahead with its prohibition, mailing a notice to all member banks on 13 December 1971 that they could not maintain dual membership. Worthen Bank and Trust responded by seeking a cease-and-desist order to prevent NBI from communicating with its members on the matter of duality unless cleared to do so by the court.

The initial battle was won by NBI, but the resourceful Worthen Bank and Trust was not yet ready to concede defeat. Its continued legal struggle with NBI resulted in a landmark decision that was a clear victory for Worthen. On 20 July, 1972, Senior Justice John E. Miller of the U.S. District Court, Eastern District of Arkansas, Western Division, held NBI to be in violation of antitrust laws and was enjoined from enforcing Bylaw 216 to prevent member banks from issuing Master Charge and BankAmericard simultaneously. The twenty-six-page opinion stated that the ability of an issuing bank to handle both cards gives it a "greatly enhanced" competitive position; the court found, therefore, that NBI's bylaws constituted restraint of trade and commerce. The ruling further defined the purpose of antitrust laws as protection for consumers from the effects of unfair competition as much as protection for businesspeople and observed that NBI's bylaw served no one's interest except its own. With this ruling, Worthen instituted its Master Charge program, which had been held in abeyance while the case was in litigation.

A month later, on 25 August, NBI began the appeal process in the Eighth Circuit Court of Appeals in St. Louis. That process would drag on for the next five years. But while the law on duality remained unsettled, a number of banks capitalized on the resulting confusion and issued both BankAmericard and Master Charge simultaneously. In 1976, mainly as a result of pressure from the Justice Department, NBI gave up its opposition to duality. That year, it approved thirty-eight BankAmericard applications from Master Charge banks. By October of that year, a number of the very largest BankAmericard banks, including Bank of America and Chase Manhattan, had applied to Interbank for Master Charge membership. With the decision of some of the largest issuers to participate, both the legality and practicality of the duality concept were settled.

It has never been clear to analysts of the financial services sector whether duality had a positive effect on competition. It certainly placed pressure on banks to sign up as many merchants as possible, since there was no reason why merchants should go to the trouble of submitting

BankAmericard sales slips to one bank and Master Charge sales slips to another. In the scramble to recruit merchant contracts, the larger banks had the advantage because they had more money to spend on sales representatives and literature and were able to offer more services to merchants than the smaller banks. Once the merchant base was locked up by the big banks, the smaller banks found it difficult to act as independents in the card business, although they could still operate as agents.

Another effect of duality was that discount rates to merchants were initially lowered as banks competed for the double charge card business. While this benefited the merchants, the gains were short-lived; discounts would be raised within a year or so.

The effect on consumers and banks was even harder to measure. The immediate impact on consumers was a stepped-up marketing campaign by banks to place a second card in the hands of all current cardholders. Almost overnight, aggregate credit lines for customers rose $15 billion nationwide. Banks were faced with a tremendous increase in the cost of marketing and processing two cards instead of one.

In September 1977, Assistant Attorney General John Shenefield of the Justice Department warned the American Bankers Association (ABA) that trends for combining Visa and Master Charge marketing and processing applications might be challenged in the courts from the standpoint that it diluted competition. Many banks had begun merging their cardholders' Visa and Master Charge billings on one statement, computing interest on combined volume, soliciting new cardholders with a combined application form, and giving merchants universal charge forms on which they could write up either Visa or Master Charge business. Now the banks were being admonished to maintain the trappings of competition while operating what was essentially a single service. Ironically, the court's 1972 ruling on duality, which then seemed to hold out the prospect of stimulating competition, was now viewed as favoring the opposite result.

With the proliferation of credit cards in the late 1970s, consumers were inundated with applications and promotional mailings for new cards. Although many people did possess several cards, it was becoming more difficult for them to sort through the many applications they received. Furthermore, it was a time-consuming process to fill out a similar credit application form for every new card. Several innovative promotional plans aimed at streamlining the application process were formed. One particularly effective one introduced by Timesavers Group of Washington, D.C., was the Timesaver program. Recognizing the well-known propensity of individuals to own a multitude of cards, the

Timesaver combined applications for a sizable number of T&E, airline travel, auto rental, and gasoline cards into a single form. An applicant could apply for as many cards as he or she wished. Despite its convenience, the Timesaver plan has not been widely used since its introduction in 1974.

In 1979, the strain of the marketing war finally began to show. Early that year, Chase Manhattan Bank dropped its Master Charge operation. At the time, Chase was the nation's third-largest bank card issuer, with over 2.8 million Visa cards outstanding, but it had found duality so unprofitable that it discontinued Master Charge. Holders of Chase Master Charge cards were invited to convert their accounts to Visa.

International Markets

The growth of the bank cards domestically during the 1970s was paralleled by their growth internationally. Throughout this decade, both BankAmericard and Master Charge aggressively marketed their cards throughout Europe and in Asia. Their dogged pursuit of franchising agreements with foreign merchants and banks mirrored the fierce competition between the two networks in the domestic market. As in the United States, Master Charge enjoyed the initial advantage, but Bank Americard was moving quickly to close the gap.

The licensing of BankAmericard franchises outside of the United States had been initiated in 1966; franchises spread to fifty-two countries under licensing agreements directly with the Bank of America. By 1972, BankAmericard International was operating in seventy-one countries. It had affiliations with nearly 15,000 banks and banking offices and had signed up 250,000 merchant outlets and 6.2 million cardholders, who generated nearly $700 million in sales. However, with the exception of its Barclay Card operation in Great Britain, BankAmericard's coverage was poor in Europe.

In the early 1970s, Interbank had much better prospects for expanding its Master Charge international operations into Europe, partly because of the European banks' fear of aligning themselves with BankAmericard and its namesake and principal member, Bank of America, the world's largest bank. There was also a considerable amount of anti-American sentiment in Europe at that time because of the war in Vietnam. Interbank, with its much lower, and less openly American, profile was much more appealing. In 1974, it gained a distinct advantage over BankAmericard in Europe when it signed an agreement with Great

Britain's Access card to bolster agreements it had been signing with affiliates of EuroCard.

EuroCard had been formed in 1965 through the merger of two competing T&E cards: the Rikskort card of Sweden, which was owned by the Wallenberg family, and the BHR card issued by the British Hotel and Restaurant Association. EuroCard International (ECI), which owns the EuroCard trademark and logo, was headquartered in Sweden and served as the coordinating body of the system. It was jointly owned by EuroCard Deutschland, Access of Great Britain, EuroCard France, and the Wallenberg family of Sweden. Revolving credit was not made available to most EuroCard holders. The amounts charged were automatically debited to the customer's bank account each month. As part of its agreement with EuroCard, Interbank processed all EuroCard charges through its clearing network.

Access was issued by Great Britain's Joint Credit Card Company, which consisted of National Westminster, Midland, and Lloyd's Bank. In 1974, Joint Credit Card finally agreed to join Interbank, a major coup for Interbank. At that time, Great Britain was by far the largest credit card market in Europe, and the second-largest in the world after the United States. Access was then the second-largest card in Great Britain (behind BankAmericard's affiliate Barclay Card), with over 3.2 million cardholders and 84,000 merchant outlets. More importantly, according to the *Financial Times* of London (1974), Access was also growing more rapidly than its rival.

As a result of their agreement, as well as Joint Credit Card's reciprocal agreement with EuroCard, new Access cards displayed the Interbank symbol on the front in addition to carrying both the Master Charge and EuroCard symbols on the back. Over the next five years, Access would overtake and pass Barclay Card in the size of its cardholder base. By 1979, Access had more than double the number of cardholders of Barclay Card, with 3.7 million cards in circulation to Barclay's 1.8 million.

Although it was losing the battle in Great Britain, BankAmericard refused to give up the international war with Master Charge. In 1974, it formed Ibanco to administer BankAmericard abroad. The charter members of Ibanco included banks from Canada, Colombia, Greece, Italy, Japan, Lebanon, Mexico, Portugal, Puerto Rico, Spain, South Africa, Great Britain, the United States, and Venezuela. Common to all cards issued by Ibanco members was a blue, white, and gold band designed and originated by Bank of America in 1958 and subsequently licensed to other banks and bank card centers throughout the United States and abroad. The organization was initially funded by service fees equal to

0.8 percent of each member's sales volume plus usage fees for specific services such as international draft interchange.

In 1976, as a sign of its growing commitment to internationalizing its operations, NBI changed the name of its credit card from BankAmericard to Visa, a word recognized and understood in countries around the world. Thereafter, BankAmericard would be used by Bank of America only for its California customers. The name change was not inexpensive, costing some $9.2 million to display the Visa logo in two million retail establishments in 110 countries and in 7,500 card-issuing and agent banks. Visa signs replaced not only BankAmericard but also Chargex, Barclay Card, Carte Bleue, Banco Credito, Bank Union, Sumitomocard, and other foreign cards. In the conversion process, NBI paid McLean County Bank of Bloomington, Illinois, $10,000 to settle a trademark dispute over the name Visa. Four years later, in 1980, Interbank would follow Visa's lead by changing the name of its card from Master Charge to the more international-sounding MasterCard, allocating $11 million to promote the newly designed card.

Despite Master Charge's early lead internationally, Visa (with the aforementioned exception of Great Britain) eventually overtook its rival. In Israel, for example, Interbank was the first to gain access to the market when it reached an agreement in 1975 with Isracard, which was issued by the Bank Haopalim banking group. But Visa gained considerable ground in Israel when Bank Leumi acquired the Israeli Diners Club operation and used it to launch its Visa-affiliated Leumi-Card in 1979.

That same year saw Visa also holding a comfortable lead over Master Charge in Spain—where its affiliate Banco de Bilbao had 1.5 million cards in circulation, compared with the approximately 500,000 cards issued by the Master Charge consortium of sixteen major Spanish Banks—and in France, where its affiliate Carte Bleue dominated the field with 700,000 cards issued. Visa also had gained a superior position in Japan, which by the end of the decade had pulled into second place worldwide in the number of credit cards issued. By 1977, Visa-affiliated cards in Japan outnumbered Master Charge cards two to one.

One market that proved particularly difficult for both companies to enter was Sweden. In 1980, Sweden ranked ninth in the world in credit cards, with 4.6 million outstanding. However, less than 20 percent of these cards, some 900,000, were universal credit cards. Most were debit cards used to access ATMs or cash dispensers, retail cards, or gas cards. The growth of bank and T&E cards was hindered by consumer credit laws that excluded cards as a payment mechanism.

Another notable aspect of the Swedish credit card system was the presence of a large-scale private-label program for retailers. An independent credit card operation, for a fee, issued a credit card bearing the name of the retailer. The retailer could enjoy the advantages of a private credit card, such as maintaining customer loyalty and being able to offer the card at a lower cost, without the expense of running such a large operation.

Although never very successful in the United States, where it was less expensive for larger retailers to operate their own credit card operations and for smaller retailers to accept bank cards, in Sweden the private-label concept was made profitable by a single credit card pioneer, Erik Elinder. Through Elinder's efforts, his company, Inter Conto, made private-label operations a viable alternative. Inter Conto's relationship with more than 1,500 retail stores across Sweden prompted Visa to reach an agreement with it in 1977 to sign up Swedish merchants. Visa cards were first issued by Inter Conto in 1978; as part of the agreement, Inter Conto was allowed to retain its own name in the blue band on the face of the card. This agreement marked the first time an entity other than a bank was allowed to issue Visa cards in Europe.

Invading the Department Stores

As the marketing war between Visa and Master Charge reached its peak, both companies began to explore a number of new programs to increase their cardholder base. Their efforts often bypassed the banks entirely, particularly their efforts to break into the retail market, the last significant market offering hope for expansion.

The bank card companies had pursued the larger retailers throughout the 1970s. The major stumbling block, as it had always been, was the perceived loss of identity by retailers who gave up their own cards. To overcome this perception, a number of companies developed a compromise plan, the "custom" card: it satisfied retailers by carrying their identification, while giving the bank card companies access to the retail market.

Prior to 1978, the custom business had been dominated by Citicorp Credit Services, General Electric Credit Corporation, and the National Data Corporation. Realizing the opportunity that it was missing by not allowing nonfinancial companies to have a bank card that retained their identity, Visa began to experiment with a custom credit card. It began in 1978 with a card for Pay-n-Save stores in Seattle that carried both the Visa and Pay-n-Save names. Then Bank of America arranged for Budget Rent-A-Car to issue Visa cards.

Although Budget, like the other car rental companies, issued a corporate card for centralized billing of corporate customers, it had never issued a consumer card similar to those issued by the larger car rental companies. Instead, it had chosen to honor American Express, Visa, Master Charge, Diners Club, Carte Blanche, UATP, and a few others, including the Sears card. Although a nonmember, Budget approached Bank of America to explore the feasibility of issuing a Visa card bearing its mark in the blue band of the card. Bank of America agreed to run Budget's Visa program on a custom card basis for a fee. The cards would be owned by Bank of America, which would also assume the liability for them.

The development of custom credit cards took a bizarre turn toward the end of 1978 when both the Democratic and Republican parties considered setting up arrangements with banks to issue Visa or Master Charge cards with the party's name on the back. The Democratic party proposed adding the donkey's head to the front and the slogan "United in Victory" to the reverse side of the card. It planned to send letters to Democratic party members urging them to visit certain banks to sign up for the card. The party's reward would be either a fee for each card issued or a percentage of sales.

The plans of the political parties were undermined somewhat when Senator William Proxmire protested bank cards being promoted to those on political lists. As chairman of the Senate Banking, Housing, and Urban Affairs Committee, he called a hearing to investigate the propriety of the Republican and Democratic national committees' proposals to raise campaign funds from fees on party members who accepted a Visa or Master Charge card.

After conducting meetings with representatives of both the Republican and Democratic national committees, Senator Proxmire called political party credit card promotions "cheap hucksterism," and on 25 January 1979 introduced Senate Bill 217, which would prohibit the use of bank card funds for political fund-raising. The bill died in committee.

In the summer of 1979, Bank of America set up a private label for a shopping card in San Jose. It was a cooperative venture for over one hundred merchants in the El Paseo de Saratoga shopping complex, where many upper-class specialty shops competed with Penney and other retail chains in the nearby Westgate Shopping Center. From a historical perspective, the El Paseo de Saratoga Shopping card was a rather interesting development because it resembled quite closely the local area bank card introduced by John Biggins at the Flatbush National Bank in Brooklyn some twenty years before.

Although the custom cards provided access to part of the retail market, the bulk still remained beyond the bank card companies' grasp. By the late 1970s, however, the tremendous growth of the industry was making it ever more difficult for the larger retailers to keep bank cards out. By 1978, bank cards had become "big business." Nearly fifty-two million Americans owned at least two bank cards that they used to ring up some $44 billion in annual sales—or 31 percent of total credit card spending, just shy of the volume on retail store cards, which accounted for 34 percent of credit card volume.

With the expanded credit limits, the buying power of bank cardholders could no longer be ignored by many retail establishments, particularly by the last major holdout, the department store, which had long used its proprietary card as a means of building sales and customer loyalty. (A few stores used retail cards to generate profits, but that practice was far from the norm.) The larger retailers were united in their belief that their hold on the customer would be broken if customers could use bank cards as well as retail cards. In addition, since credit card operations produced significant economies of scale, sharing credit sales with the banks would make the store credit operations even more costly. On the flip side was the potential business from millions of potential customers who were more likely to possess a bank card than a particular store's charge card.

The Visa–Penney Accord

Among the most difficult retailers to crack were the "big three" department stores—Sears, J. C. Penney, and Montgomery Ward. Each operated thousands of stores nationwide, and all three had credit operations that individually rivaled the bank cards. The bank card companies had spent years trying to break into this large market, but with no success.

Finally, in April 1979, Visa stunned the credit industry when it announced the signing of a contract with J. C. Penney. Most industry analysts believed that, if any one of the big three capitulated to the bank cards, the other two would probably be forced to accept them sooner or later. The agreement, however, angered many Visa member banks because it bypassed them, allowing J. C. Penney to deal directly with Visa and depriving the banks of any merchant discount.

This marked the beginning of a realization by many banks that the bank card companies that they had nurtured and ostensibly owned had become, by the beginning of the 1980s, uncontrollable competitors. Although nominally controlled by the banks, the bank card companies were able to function autonomously. Because the member banks were so numerous, they did not have a direct supervisory relationship with the bank card companies.

In July 1979, Sears began to experiment with accepting bank cards, following the example set by J. C. Penney several months earlier. Sears began by honoring both Visa and Master Charge cards in eleven stores in the Milwaukee area and followed up with similar tests on each coast in the fall of 1979. But it never expanded its acceptance nationwide. Very quickly, it became apparent that the feared takeover of retail credit cards would never materialize. By 1981, seventy-five of the country's largest department stores accepted some kind of third-party card, but only forty-eight accepted bank cards. In fact, American Express was more successful at penetrating this market, primarily because it was less of a threat to the retailers' own cards.

Ironically, just as the bank cards were savoring their victory in breaking into the retail market, oil companies, which had begun honoring bank cards several years earlier, were making plans to drop them. Except for a short period during the gasoline shortage of 1973, oil companies had accepted bank cards throughout the 1970s. By 1978, 26 percent of the 117 billion gallons of gasoline sold for passenger car use in the United States was charged to credit cards, and over half of the $20.6 billion in credit sales were made on Visa or Master Charge.

The oil companies were learning, however, that there was a high price to pay for the bank card business in the form of merchants' fees— $63 million in 1978 alone. Because of the increasing use of bank cards for gasoline, it was anticipated that by 1985 oil companies would be spending $695 million annually for merchant discounts on bank cards used for gasoline purchases. The bank card companies were a "partner" that many oil companies no longer wanted, but competition forced them to continue accepting bank cards. Once again, they were saved by a gas shortage, this time owing to oil restrictions that followed in the wake of the 1979 Iranian crisis. Soon after, several oil companies stopped accepting bank cards.

The Thrift Industry

The focus of this chapter, thus far, has been on the development and distribution of credit cards by commercial banks. The distinction between banks and thrift institutions such as savings and loan associations (S&Ls), mutual savings banks, and credit unions is no longer clear, but only recently so.

The 1970s, which saw major developments in bank cards, also saw a parallel and not unrelated development in the expanding powers of thrift institutions, which showed both the willingness and ability to compete head-on with banks in a full range of financial services. Beginning in 1972 in Massachusetts, negotiable orders of withdrawal (NOW) accounts, which enabled thrift customers to write checklike instruments and receive interest on their accounts, spread throughout New England and to bordering states through congressionally authorized expansion of NOW account powers. In a similar action, many credit unions throughout the United States began offering share drafts—which are interest-paying demand deposits—to their members.

It is remarkable that thrift institutions were kept out of the bank card industry until 1973, partly as the result of restrictive laws and partly as the result of resistance from the commercial banks. On 18 October 1973, NBI amended its bylaws to make mutual savings banks eligible for Class A and B membership. Following legislation in Massachusetts and Oregon authorizing mutual savings banks to issue and honor credit cards, BankAmericard added five mutual savings banks as Class A members in 1974. The first mutual banks to join NHI were Home Savings of Boston and City Savings of Pittsfield, Massachusetts. Interbank did not vote to accept mutual savings banks until 21 February 1974.

Credit unions were forced to enter the bank card field through the back door, by means of a member bank. In 1975, the Minneapolis-based Teacher Federation Credit Union offered its 7,600 members a credit card through the Marquette Bank. One problem faced by the credit unions, however, was the 12 percent limitation on credit charges imposed by law on federally chartered credit unions and applied as well to many state-chartered associations. In 1977, State Savings and Loan of Stockton, California, became the first S&L in the nation to be granted a proprietary license for bank cards, having been accepted by Visa. Other S&Ls had been issuing Visa and Master Charge cards in Michigan and Maryland, but they did not have a proprietary license.

When the S&Ls and credit unions launched their credit card plans in earnest in 1977, most offered interest rates substantially below those offered by the commercial banks. For example, the Stockton, California State Savings and Loan Association offered a 12 percent annual rate. As a result, it opened 3,000 new accounts in the first sixty days.

The S&Ls were responsible for a number of profitable innovations. A system used by state S&Ls was to approve a credit limit of up to 50 percent of the amount on deposit, which had to be held as security. Another innovation first used by state S&Ls and later by many other types of thrift institutions was to eliminate the float on finance charges and to charge every purchaser interest from the date of purchase with no "free ride."

In July 1977, the nation's largest S&L, Home Savings and Loan Association of California, was accepted as a card-issuing member of Visa. Since Home's objective was to get more money in savings, it set up a $5,000 minimum passbook requirement. In addition, the Visa card became a debit card: charges had to be paid in full in thirty days or the unpaid balance would be taken from savings at the end of the billing period. The strategy of the thrifts was to charge a lower finance rate but to charge it to all customers, thus capturing the profitable credit-using market from the banks and leaving the banks with the more affluent "free riders" who did not contribute to the cost of running the operation.

The growth of the bank card industry in the 1970s was phenomenal. Almost overnight, the banks transformed both the credit card industry and the consumer marketplace. Once reserved for only businesspeople and the wealthy, credit cards were now carried by nearly half of all American consumers. Expansion was not confined to the United States; the banks quickly learned, as did the T&E cards before them, that the credit card was a readily exportable financial service, and companies scrambled to secure a portion of the worldwide markets.

With growth came consolidation, which, in an industry so dependent upon size and economies of scale, seems to have been an inevitable development. By the end of the decade, a relatively small number of banks issued a majority of the bank credit cards. The cards that they issued were, with few exceptions, either Visa or MasterCard. Although nominally controlled by their member banks, the two bank card companies effectively operated as independent entities. Their competition was a major focus of the 1970s. Although MasterCard held the advantage initially, it was eventually passed by its rival in 1979. By 1985 Visa led MasterCard by nearly one-third, with 86.4 million cardholders to MasterCard's 64.9 million. Since most banks issue both cards and nearly all merchants accept both, many have again raised the question of why banks need to support the overhead for both organizations, much of which involves advertising against each other. Should Visa continue to extend its lead in the coming years, this question will certainly be a serious consideration for many banks and merchants.

5

Growing Pains:
Legal and
Operational Problems

By ANY STANDARDS, THE GROWTH OF THE
credit card industry in the 1970s was remarkable. This growth did not
come easily, however; legal and operational problems abounded. The
majority of the legal questions were the natural consequence of a previously unregulated industry suddenly reaching a point where it had to be
controlled both for its own good and for the public good. Similarly, many
of the operational problems encountered by the credit card companies
were the result of too much growth too quickly. Unlike the computer
industry, which has always been technology-driven—that is, the technology available predates possible applications—the credit card industry in
the 1970s was rich in ideas but lacked the technology to implement them
at a reasonable cost. The industry would have to endure a period of high
costs and processing problems until the technology could be developed.

Legal Issues

At the start of the 1970s, the most pressing problems for the credit
card companies were legal ones. While the banks had expected to
encounter operational and other business-related problems, they were
not as prepared to deal with the legal issues spawned by the industry's
expansion. But as the credit card became a familiar and necessary part
of everyday life, basic questions such as equal access and privacy

needed to be addressed. Increased government intervention and regulation were inevitable.

During the early years of the credit card industry, separate legislation relating to the cards had never been deemed necessary. Since the original function of the credit card was to identify the possessor of a charge account, fraudulent use of it was covered under existing statues relating to fraud. Later, when the revolving credit feature was added to the cards, state laws governing interest charges sufficed. It was not until the late 1960s, when the various credit card companies had jelled into an "industry" through the sharing of common features, that legislation could really be directed at the use of credit cards per se.

The event that triggered the first round of legal problems for the credit card industry in the 1970s was the same event that had initiated its rapid growth—mailings of unsolicited credit cards. In addition to swelling the ranks of cardholders, these mailings also generated numerous complaints from consumers. As problems mounted, the government finally intervened. In 1970, after a temporary suspension by the Federal Trade Commission of such mailings, President Richard Nixon stepped in and banned the practice entirely.

In their haste to acquire cardholders, banks frequently did not take the time to screeen customers carefully before issuing cards. Not surprisingly, a number of mistakes resulted, both comical and costly. It was not so much the fact that the cards were occasionally sent to children or dogs (which they were) or that they were intercepted and used illegally (which they were) that prompted the government to ban the mailings. Rather, it was the unwillingness and/or inability of the banks to protect their customers from the effects of these mistakes that made the practice into a political issue and forced the government to clamp down on it.

If an unsolicited card was intercepted and misused, the first indication of the theft might be a bill for thousands of dollars received by an individual who had neither requested nor wanted a credit card. Although the individual was theoretically protected from that loss by existing laws, the responsibility was placed upon him or her to prove innocence. When that individual was subsequently billed by the card company for the fraudulent charges, the bank would try to collect on the debt, forcing the individual to try to prove that he or she had never made the charges. While this battle might be won in court, it was an expensive and time-consuming process.

Some banks might have thought that the banning of mailings of unsolicited cards marked the end of government intervention and legal wrangling. Unfortunately, it was only the beginning. The mailings had opened a Pandora's box of legal questions that had to be answered if the industry was to continue to grow. The primary areas of concern were:

☐ *Lost or stolen cards:* In just a few hours, a professional criminal could ring up several thousands of dollars in charges with a lost or stolen credit card, long before he or she could be discovered. Who was not liable for those charges? The customer who had lost the card? The bank that had issued it? Or the merchant who had allowed the fraudulent charges to be made?

☐ *Billing errors:* As the sudden dramatic increase in transactions quickly overtaxed existing processing systems, billing errors multiplied at a tremendous rate. The consumer whose bill was in error could be forced to take on a giant bank to resolve a dispute. To make the odds more uneven, that same bank might also control the consumer's bank account and could freeze or take funds from the account prior to the resolution of the problem. Who would protect the consumer? Who would oversee the resolution of such cases?

☐ *Equal access:* As the credit card became a necessity of everyday life, it became an economic "right" of all Americans. Which laws and regulations ensured equal access, and who enforced those laws? Once a consumer started using a credit card and companies began to compile a credit history, who would protect that consumer's right to privacy regarding this information?

Other more tangential legal issues also had to be addressed. For example, the question of usury came to the forefront in the 1970s as market interest rates pushed up the cost of funds to the card companies. While that problem applied to all types of consumer credit, separate legislation had to be designed for the specific billing procedures used by the credit card companies.

Both the government and the courts struggled with these questions throughout the 1970s. Eventually, they established a body of case precedents—laws and regulations to answer the various questions and to govern the expanding industry.

One of the first problems tackled was the nuts-and-bolts issue of billing disputes. On 27 April 1972, Congress passed the Fair Credit Billing Act, which gave the Federal Reserve Board broad discretion to regulate billing practices. It also mandated a sixty-day period for consumers to make written complaints of billing errors and a fifteen-day period for card issuers to acknowledge receipt, followed by sixty days for investigation, correction, or explanation by the card issuer.

Over the next three years, continuing examination of the credit card industry led to various revisions of this act. The final version, which was passed into law on 28 October 1975, added regulations to cover disputes over shoddy or defective merchandise purchased with a credit card. The act specified that a consumer could send the credit card company a written notification of errors made in card billing, including charges for shoddy or defective merchandise. If notification was made within sixty days of the billing, credit card companies were obliged to acknowledge that notification within thirty days and to resolve the dispute within two complete billing cycles. The act also required the card companies to provide cardholders with a statement of cardholders' rights twice each year and to get bills into their hands at least fourteen days before the end of the billing period.

Another issue that the act addressed centered on the relationship between the merchant and the credit card company. In April 1974, BankAmericard and American Express had been forced to settle out of court a suit brought against them by Consumers Union. The suit charged the credit card companies with violation of antitrust laws, based on their prohibition on merchants offering cash discounts to non–credit card users. As part of the settlement, American Express notified its merchants that they "may grant discounts for cash payments with respect to some or all merchandise or services if the discount is clearly and conspicuously offered to all cash customers." This practice was codified in the final version of the Fair Credit Billing Act, which expressly guaranteed the right of merchants to offer discounts to cash customers.

Equal Credit Opportunity

While the problems of resolving billing disputes were fairly straightforward, the issue of granting fair and equal access to credit was both much more complicated and much vaster in scope. On a practical level, the issue of access revolved around the question of what information could or could not be used in deciding whether to grant a prospective customer credit. The primary question was whether an applicant was likely to have his or her civil rights violated by the disclosure of certain "protected" characteristics such as race, sex, or marital status on a credit application. An applicant's civil rights had to be weighed against the credit card company's need for such information to inform its judgment of the applicant's creditworthiness. (A side issue that arose during this debate was whether regulatory authorities could even monitor compliance with antidiscrimination laws without collecting such information.

After agreements were made with civil rights organizations, the information was collected on certain consumer credit applications, such as mortgages, by the relevant federal agencies so that they could monitor compliance.)

With the relatively low profit margin of most credit card plans, credit investigations had to be handled economically. Most of the information about an applicant was obtained from the application. The credit card company then added other verifiable information and determined the criteria for acceptance.

Initially, the bank card companies had structured their selection process to minimize credit loss. However, they soon discovered that this practice simply generated a customer list that included a large proportion of unprofitable "free riders"—those who paid their bills on time and, therefore, did not pay interest. Eventually the card companies adjusted their selection process to include customers who would establish a profitable relationship with them. The profile of a "profitable" customer was someone with a good credit history that showed an extensive use of revolving credit, timely payments, and a record of steady employment. Such a customer was considered a much more profitable prospect than a wealthy person who avoided paying interest by always paying off the entire outstanding balance at the end of each payment period.

Applicant information was processed in two ways. The low-tech method was using human judgment to weigh the various factors. If, for example, an applicant had both an unfavorable factor, such as irregular income, and a favorable factor, such as job stability, the analyst would use his or her own judgment in weighing those factors. This method was fairer, but it was also more expensive than an automated procedure and less adaptable to centralized control.

The second method was to apply an explicit set of weights to each factor. These weights were multiplied by each factor and the products added together to obtain a score—hence the term "credit scoring." A number of vendors specialized in supplying credit scoring systems to credit card issuers. If the issuer was large enough and had been in business for a while, its own past experience was used to establish the weights. If it was small or new, industry average weights were used, at least initially. Credit scoring systems not only gave accept/reject recommendations, but also often helped establish the size of an applicant's credit line. More sophisticated companies used a variant of the credit scoring system to increase or decrease credit lines over time.

In spite of the efficiency of credit scoring systems, civil rights groups consistently opposed them as being inherently discriminatory.

Many variables that aided the predictive power of the credit scoring model related to personal, noneconomic characteristics of applicants such as race, sex, age, and marital status. Some individuals who would ordinarily have qualified for credit might have been rejected because of personal characteristics over which they had no control.

Another aspect of the credit application process that elicited objections from civil rights groups in 1979 was "redlining." Redlining was using the location of residence as a factor in deciding whether to allow or reject a credit application. Critics argued that the classification of an applicant by neighborhood could be a proxy for factors that are not allowed in the credit scoring model, such as race or national origin. They also pointed out that the use of neighborhood to characterize an applicant would, as the term implies, be painting all of the residents of particular neighborhoods with the same brush, a sort of "guilt by proximity." A bill to prohibit credit card companies from using zip codes in their credit scoring systems was introduced in 1979 as Senate Bill S15 by Carl Levin. The bill did not pass the Senate.

Several banks also attempted to lower the cost of checking applicant credit records through prescreening. One method was using what was called a "score yourself" application form, which had a point scoring system on the face of the application: points were given for factors such as age, marital status, dependents, years at present address, monthly income, years with present employer, and education. If the applicant scored more than sixteen points, he or she was urged to complete the application and submit it.

On 28 October 1975, Congress enacted the first Equal Credit Opportunity Act. It ensured each citizen's right to a fair opportunity to secure credit. Its cost to lenders for revised application forms and procedures was estimated by James F. Smith of the Federal Reserve Board, in an article published in 1977, to approach $300 million.

The final version of the bill, which became effective 23 March 1977, contained provisions that not only prohibited the use of personal information such as sex, race, national origin, and marital status as criteria for selection, but also required all lenders taking adverse action on credit applications to notify applicants in writing and state specifically why such action was taken. In its enforcement of the new act, the Federal Reserve did not forbid the use of credit scoring systems but suggested that some standardized level of reliability be used. If, for example, it could be shown statistically that 95 percent of applicants with scores above a certain level did, in fact, make payments on time, the rejection of individuals with scores below that point could be supported. If, however, an applicant could prove that the scoring system resulted in a wrongful denial of credit, that person could sue for damages, including damages on behalf of his or her class.

In a related move, Congress, at the behest of the Federal Reserve Board, followed the recommendations of the U.S. Civil Rights Commission and included in the Equal Credit Opportunity Act the provision that women should be allowed to have credit bureau files maintained in their own names. Many women who became divorced or widowed found that their credit record disappeared and that they were treated as new borrowers, with all the limitations of that status. Other women who had been married to irresponsible borrowers found that the status of their former spouses stayed with them.

Privacy

The last major legal hurdle that the bank card companies had to clear was the question of privacy. The transformation of payment systems from the use of currency to a transfer of credits and debits by necessity entailed some loss of privacy for the transactors. When purchases are made by check, privacy is not a serious issue. But checks are most often written for larger, planned expenditures, while credit cards are most frequently used for impulsive purchases. My own studies and those of others have shown that credit cards tend to be used in place of cash, not checks. The implication is that a great many transactions for which privacy is desired have never been handled by check but rather by cash and, more recently, by credit card.

The difference in the processes also caused users to be more concerned with invasion of privacy through credit cards than through checks. The need to authorize a great many credit card purchases and to keep records on-line, in addition to the need for access to slips to check errors, made credit card files more readily accessible to a larger number of individuals than checking account files. Furthermore, by the 1970s, privacy in general was a much more important concern for most people than it had been when checking accounts were first being developed. It is much easier to build safeguards into a new system than to retrofit them to an old one.

To many, the arch villain in the privacy debate appeared to be the credit bureaus whose responsibility it was to maintain active files on the creditworthiness of as many Americans as possible. Credit bureaus were routinely besieged by police departments, mailing list companies, and even employers for information on individuals. In the early 1970s, Ralph Nader attacked the Retail Credit Company of Atlanta and the

Capital Credit Data Corporation for keeping files on seventy-two million Americans who do not know their lives are being checked into. Nader stated that Retail Credit alone had files on forty-five million people while Capital Credit kept track of twenty-seven million and was adding seven million new names each year. He also pointed out that the government routinely used credit bureau information as part of its investigations of individuals, observing that "some credit firms found it was the better part of valor to share files with the government."

Another aspect of the privacy issue concerned the sale and use of credit card mailing lists. While thousands of other mailing lists of certain consumers, such as magazine subscribers and airplane pilots, were routinely sold, many felt that the sale of a list of those who qualified for a credit card fell into a special category. For this reason, the FTC investigated in 1971 the rental of credit card lists by American Express, Carte Blanche, and Diners Club. Although the bank card companies were not direct targets of the investigation, they were keenly interested in its outcome. A decision to ban the renting of cardholder lists would cost them hundreds of thousands of dollars in annual revenue. The FTC found that, for 1970, American Express had earned approximately $850,000, Diners Club $264,000, and Carte Blanche $90,000, through the rental of cardholder lists. Ultimately, the FTC declined to press charges against any of the companies cited.

In 1973, American Express was named, along with *Playboy, Esquire, Time*, and *Ladies' Home Journal*, in a $50 million class action suit involving the release of customer mailing lists. In 1974, as the result of pressure from that suit and the FTC, as well as cardholder complaints, American Express notified its cardholders that they could opt to have their names deleted from mailing lists that the company rented or sold in the future. Surprisingly, less than one percent of the cardholders took American Express up on its offer. That response was partly attributable to the public's indifference to the issue—many people simply do not care if they receive junk mail or not. Furthermore, many people do not read notices sent by credit card companies unless they relate to the bill. Consequently, only a small number of people ask to have their names removed from mailing lists, the sale of which continues to be a profitable venture today, although it is now handled by the card-issuing banks, not Visa and MasterCard.

In 1974, the Federal Privacy Act became law. It established the Privacy Protection Study Commission, which lasted from June 1975 to December 1977 and began investigating credit card systems in 1976. The commission, initially headed by Carole W. Parsons, was particularly concerned with information that could individually identify consumers. Commission members wanted to know the type and form of information that was collected, its purpose, and sources and methods of verification. They were also interested in new technology, particularly the ways in which point-of-sale (POS) debiting generates data on consumers.

Following a Supreme Court ruling in April 1976 that bank records were not confidential under existing laws, Rep. Edward I. Koch (later the mayor of New York City) introduced a bill designed to restrict access to consumer information stored in credit bank (computer storage of credit information) or telephone toll call records. H.R. 1985, the Protection of Private Records Act, was introduced after AT&T refused to protect its phone toll call records from disclosure. Under the terms of H.R. 1985, an individual's records could be released only with his or her consent or by a court order with notice to him or her. The legislation died in committee, however. Despite their defeat on the federal level in 1977, consumer rights advocates could claim at least one victory that year: Superior Court judge Jerry Pacht ruled it illegal to rent or sell credit card mailing lists in California.

One significant conclusion reached by the Privacy Protection Study Commission was that credit card companies were lax in protecting the confidentiality of customer files. David Linowes, chairman of the commission, complained that information about the buying habits of credit customers was successfully obtained by IRS agents and other investigators through a variety of deceptive means. He alleged that 90 percent of the cases in which the government obtained information from credit card companies involved a mere phone call, with no record being kept. The commission also suggested making it more difficult for companies to use credit records in prescreening. A number of larger banks across the country commonly used prescreened lists to solicit creditworthy cardholders.

Some of the commission's recommendations were strongly opposed by the Justice Department. Legislation to ensure the confidentiality of bank customer records had the support of the American Bankers Association and the U.S. League of Savings Associations but was opposed by Benjamin R. Civaletti, then deputy attorney general, who believed that protecting confidentiality would be detrimental to law enforcement. His objections were overruled, however, when Congress passed Title XI of Public Law 95–630, the Financial Institutions Regulatory and Interest Rate Control Act of 1978. The new law was designed to prevent unauthorized access to the financial records of individuals through investigations of patterns of credit card purchases, phone calls, or check cashing. It became effective in March 1979.

Operational Problems—Controlling Costs

While the bank card companies had not expected the myriad legal problems that beset them in the 1970s, they had recognized that there would be significant operational problems in developing a national credit card operation. They were nevertheless hard-pressed to develop the technology and systems necessary to run such large operations.

One of the most difficult problems was developing an effective and cost-efficient nationwide authorization system. Such a system was important for a number of reasons. First, since cards were usable nationwide, and even worldwide, quick authorization was needed. The need for up-to-the-minute authorization information became particularly important after the debacle of the unsolicited credit card mailings. Although a negative file, or "hot list," could be circulated or accessed, delays in updating the information in it could not prevent "runaway" cards. Therefore, the ability to access information from local processing centers became critical. In addition, the relatively low credit standards used for issuing bank cards demanded tight monitoring of cardholder activity—mainly by banks rather than the T&E card companies, which had been more selective in issuing their cards and had never engaged in mass mailings.

Another use to be developed for the authorization systems was the transfer of sales information to speed the billing process. Since most banks were still losing money on their credit card operations, they were understandably anxious to assess any legitimate interest charges on cardholder purchases.

Most of these problems were solved by the development of a seemingly mundane technology called "switching." Much of the initial work on switching was done by Interbank for its Master Charge members. The creative force behind the development of Interbank's Omniswitch switching program was Edward Bontems, a pioneer in the concept of international credit card development. He was also influential in organizing the California Bank Card Association in 1966 and in developing what was then a totally new concept for a group of banks entering the charge card field—the use of the same card identity and a common computer system clearinghouse for interchange purposes. Expansion into other states led to the formation of the Western States Bank Card Association, which eventually became part of the Interbank Card Association for national and international interchange of bank charge card paper.

The interchange for credit cards functions much like the clearinghouses for checks. A credit card customer of one bank may buy something from a merchant with an account at a second bank. The interchange, in essence, returns the credit card slip to the initial bank for payment. When there are many such transactions in each direction, the interchange offsets the charges of each bank against the other.

After solving many of the operational difficulties of the bank card associations, Bontems turned his attention to the problem of credit authorization through Omniswitch. In 1970, Omniswitch operated three 360–40 IBM computers handling authorizations for five million cardholders. Among the issuers served were the Marine Midland Banks in New York and the Eastern States Bank Card Association.

Beginning in January 1972, Interbank affiliates outside of the continental United States routed their credit authorizations through Omniswitch and the Western States Bank Card Association. Omniswitch in Lake Success, New York, was a clearing point between Interbank members in the United States and affiliates in France, Great Britain, Spain, Venezuela, Colombia, and Puerto Rico. The Western States Bank Card Association in San Franciso was the clearing point for Mexico and Japan.

In May 1973, NBI made its own contribution to upgrading the system of monitoring customer reliability when it initiated its national credit authorization system. Its IBM-designed system, known as Base I, used a computer switching network providing twenty-four-hour-a-day credit authorization for BankAmericard establishments nationwide.

One major objective for both NBI and Interbank was to convert from the "country club" billing system, in which copies of original sales slips were returned to cardholders, to "descriptive" billing, in which cardholders received a computer listing of charges with no signed proof of charge. Without descriptive billing, they reasoned, the entire concept of electronic funds transfer (ETF) would flounder and profits would remain elusive. In 1973, with the exception of airline tickets, all credit card charges were processed by country club billing.

Since consumers usually wanted to see their signature on their sales slips, the card issuers anticipated considerable consumer resistance to descriptive billing. The strategy to overcome that resistance included the use of facsimile slips that resembled real slips but could be transmitted electronically. In anticipation of the move to descriptive billing, NBI implemented a Base II switching system that was designed primarily to transmit draft data between NBI issuing banks for billing purposes, eliminating the need to mail the actual copies of sales drafts created at the point of sale and allowing the initial clearing bank to retain them. This system served seventy-six large processing centers for BankAmericard banks in the United States.

The movement toward descriptive billing ended up being very gradual. Regulation Z of the Federal Reserve Board dictated that if the actual transaction slip was not enclosed, the statement had to include the date of each transaction, the amount, the seller's name, and the address of the location where the transaction took place. There was indeed some consumer resistance to descriptive billing; the common complaint was that there was no reference to the specific merchandise purchased. Descriptive billing also increased the number of customer inquiries, thereby increasing the expenses of the banks. However, it eventually proved to be a profitable move for the banks.

In November 1976, BankAmericard announced that it was expanding the capacity of its Base I/Base II authorization network. In addition to its existing operation center in San Mateo, California, NBI announced intentions to build a second center on the East Coast that was larger and technologically superior. Each was designed to handle half of the NBI credit authorization volume in the United States, but either would be capable of taking over all national and international volume if the other could not function. The original Base I system, which was designed to handle 5,000 transactions per hour with an average response time of eight seconds, could handle 16,000 per hour in under ten seconds per transaction if the merchant's signing bank had an on-line computer link to the authorization center. Authorizations were completed in as little as two seconds, with a downtime of less than one percent.

Progress in this operational area through the mid-1970s bode well for the eventual profitability of the bank card industry. However, the industry's processing problems were still not entirely behind it. In late 1978, a substantial increase in the number of bank card transactions, particularly among the larger banks, precipitated a crisis in bank card processing, and the banks were forced to significantly increase their processing capabilities. Fortunately, the technology was advancing rapidly enough to meet their needs.

At that time, First Data Resources in Omaha was the only processing center capable of handling more than 200 million transactions annually. Most of the large processing centers in the United States were running at peak capacity and were having difficulty taking care of the increased volume from their clients.

Bank card processing in 1978 fell into three categories: (1) in-house operations, used by Bank of America, Citibank, Security Pacific, Wells Fargo, Louisiana National, and most banks among the top fifty, as well as by some agressive smaller banks like Colorado National of Denver; (2) nonprofit associations such as Eastern States Monetary Services, Credit Systems Inc., the Charge Card Association, and the Southeast

Bank Card Association; and (3) independent profit-making organizations like First Data Resources. Because of the trend at that time toward "full service," bank card processing centers performed numerous duties for the banks: marketing numerous ancillary items (such as cardholder insurance, card registration and protection, mail-order merchandise, and home security protection), credit scoring, embossing and mailing, fraud investigation, security, card pickup, central fraud application files, credit authorization, and even check-cashing assistance. Additionally, bank card processing centers helped banks through the central purchasing of imprinters, forms, credit cards, and eventually, ATMs and POS terminals.

Fraud

Losses due to fraud were another major cost problem for the bank card companies. Credit card fraud was perpetrated in various ways. Usually it was accomplished through a lost or stolen card. Later, as criminals became more adept at copying the technology, they were able to reproduce cards. Perpetrators of mail fraud managed to obtain credit card numbers from unsuspecting cardholders and use that information to order goods by telephone. Some unscrupulous merchants developed a method of duplicating customer charge slips to which they added fictitious charges. All of these crimes added up to a very large bill for the bank card companies. In 1973 alone, credit card losses were estimated to be $288 million—or 1.15 percent of total credit card sales.

In the late 1960s, before the proliferation of bank cards, credit card theft was still a cottage industry, made up primarily of independent operators rather than fully organized large-scale operations. Stolen T&E and bank cards went for $200 and up in any quantity. As in most legitimate industries, as supply increased, price decreased. By 1969, stolen credit cards could be bought in batches of 100 or more in most major cities for $100 each. By 1971, small-time free-lance operators peddled them to fences for as little as $10 each. The black market price of a card depended upon how recently it had been stolen. Cards known to have been stolen less than a week before carried a premium of about 50 percent, while those that were known to have been stolen more than a week before were sold at a discount of about 50 percent from standard black market prices.

The card considered most valuable on the black market was the airline travel card, which sold for between $100 and $200—roughly twice the price of other stolen credit cards. Airline travel cards sold at such a premium because the airlines issued no warning bulletins, or hot card lists. The director of security and fraud protection at the International Air Transport Association during the early 1970s estimated airline losses to be $20 million yearly on stolen cards and tickets.

Oil company credit cards also carried a high street value—$50–100—because few station attendants checked any type of bulletin and few cards had expiration dates or signature panels. BankAmericard and Master Charge cards were sold for $50–75, Diners Club cards for $40–60, American Express for $30–50, and Carte Blanche for $20–30. The differences in price reflected the varying efficiency of the companies' security practices; Carte Blanche had the best.

Prostitutes accounted for the largest number of credit card thefts. According to the April 1971 issue of the *Nilson Report,* cards lifted by prostitutes accounted for some 40 percent of total dollar losses on cards, as compared with 35 percent from cards involved in burglaries, 15 percent from cards obtained through postal theft, and 10 percent from all others. Compounding the difficulties in apprehending the persons involved was the threat of exposure for the cardholder if he or she reported the stolen card.

Stolen cards were not the only vehicle for credit card fraud. As the legitmate use of credit cards for mail-order purchases increased in the early 1970s, criminals quickly devised ways to tap into this potentially lucrative market. The criminal would obtain the name and account number of a valid cardholder, generally through an accomplice who worked at a retail establishment where credit cards were accepted. The criminal would copy the name and account number from a valid sales slip and send it in with a temporary address, to the mail-order company. (The fraudulent use of credit card numbers to mail-order merchandise was certainly not new. In the 1960s, a prison inmate responding to advertisements in Diners Club's *Signature* magazine managed to have over $2,000 in merchandise delivered to his prison address before the cardholder whose number he was using complained of incorrect billing.)

Even some merchants became involved in credit card fraud schemes. One method that was quite common in the early 1970s was the duplication of charge slips by merchants who would forge a customer's signature, copying it from the original slip. The duplicated slip would be put through and collection would be made. This ploy was seldom noticed by the cardholder because it corresponded to an actual purchase. Sometime later, the merchant would put through the original, valid slip, and even if the cardholder noticed it, he or she would have a difficult time proving the overcharge because the legitimate signature would be on the slip.

In early 1972, BankAmericard reported its annual fraud losses to be 0.32 percent of liquidations (cardholder payments, charge-offs, and credits). To reduce the contribution of merchants to this figure, Ralph Dunker, head of security for NBI, developed a reporting system that separated fraud from interchange and noninterchange statistics. Prior to this time, merchants who were knowledgeable about the reporting system would confine their credit card fraud attempts to cards issued by interchange banks. Thus, the periodic reports on a merchant's bank card activity would not show fraud because interchange fraud was not attributed to the merchant. With the new system, NBI hoped to be able to spot merchants who were active or who conspired with criminals attempting to defraud the credit card companies.

☐ **Counterfeiting**   The first reported case of counterfeiting credit cards was made public by the Los Angeles Police Department in 1971. The counterfeiters, two women and one man, apparently used authentic blank card stock and had knowledge of at least one bank's official numbering system. Their mistake was printing embossed numerals that differed from the standard font.

Stolen cards could also be counterfeited by flattening them with an ordinary iron and reembossing them by machine, which effectively prevented them from being checked on hot card lists. Some criminals also obtained blank card stock and used valid names and account numbers; the fraudulent use of these cards was seldom detected before substantial losses had occurred, simply because the cards did not appear on hot card lists.

The most difficult counterfeit cards to detect—and therefore the most damaging in terms of losses—were "shave and paste" cards. Criminals shaved off embossed characters with razor blades and pasted them back on in different configurations so that phony names and account numbers could get through the system. There was no defense from this type of fraud as long as charges were processed from imprinted charge slips.

Another major potential source of credit card fraud were the hundreds of thousands of credit cards inadvertently left behind in retail stores and gasoline stations. In 1973, it was estimated that in the United States some thirty-five million credit cards were left behind every year. Although nearly two-thirds of the lost cards were retrieved by the rightful owners, returned to them by merchants, or destroyed, some fifteen million pieces of "plastic money" were left in circulation each year and could have been used for fraudulent purchases.

One form of fraud that had dire implications for EFT systems was tampering with data files. On 13 October 1976, six persons were convicted by a Los Angeles federal court jury of tampering with the credit data files of the world's largest databank, TRW. They worked in collusion with a TRW file cleck to alter poor credit ratings so that they could obtain bank loans and use credit cards for which they might not otherwise qualify. They erased negative entries from some credit ratings while adding favorable information to others.

The problem of data manipulation was not unique to credit cards. It was already being done with checking and other types of accounts and loans. The solution in all cases was better screening of employees and electronic auditing procedures.

In 1973, the *Nilson Report* ranked credit card security hazards by volume of dollar losses in the industry for that year. The major sources of loss were (1) stolen cards, (2) lost and misplaced cards, (3) postal theft, (4) fraudulent charges by merchants and their employees, (5) collusion between merchants and cardholders, (6) fraudulent applications, (7) mail-order telephone fraud, (8) theft from manufacturing, embossing, and mailing services, (9) alteration of cards by flattening and reembossing or substituting pictures, (10) counterfeits, and (11) magnetic stripe tampering.

☐ **The Fight against Fraud**   The fight against fraud has been carried out on many fronts through the cooperation of credit card issuers with federal, state, and local law enforcement officials. Initially, federal laws governing credit card fraud allowed for a $10,000 fine, or five years in jail, or both, on conviction of the use of a fraudulent credit card provided that the loss exceeded an aggregate minimum of $5,000. A fraudulent credit card was defined as one that was counterfeit, fictitious, altered, forged, lost, stolen, or fraudulently obtained. In October 1974, federal prosecution of credit card fraud was greatly expanded when President Gerald Ford signed a new law lowering the minimum total value of interstate and foreign credit card crime for which the United States could prosecute from $5,000 to $1,000. Penalties for credit card crimes were also stiffened: the maximum sentence was doubled from five to ten years.

During the mass mailings of the late 1960s and early 1970s, the U.S. Post Office played a significant role in law enforcement efforts against credit card fraud, in large part because of the numerous instances of credit card theft inside post offices. During the fiscal year ending in 1972, postal inspectors investigated 1,128 mail-related cases of theft and fraudulent use of credit cards, resulting in 436 convictions. Ninety-eight percent of all cases brought to trial ended in convictions.

While theft of credit cards from post offices had been a serious problem, by the early 1970s the problem was minimal.

The credit card companies also had their own volunteer law enforcement unit to fight credit card fraud—the Association of Credit Card Investigators (ACCI). However, the bulk of their efforts were focused on two areas: prevention of theft, and alerting merchants and member banks of cards that had been stolen. The companies experimented with various methods of preventing theft. Several attempts were made to affix a photograph of each cardholder to his or her card, which would render it useless to a thief. That project proved both costly and ineffective and was eventually abandoned.

One measure, initiated by Manufacturers Hanover Trust in 1970, that did prove effective was a combination of a post-mailer with dual dating on the credit card. The post-mailer informed the intended cardholder that a card had been mailed to him or her and that the credit card company should be notified if it had not yet been received. Dual dating, which had a starting date as well as an expiration date embossed on the card, enabled the credit card company to delay the effective starting date of the card until after it should have been received by the cardholder.

After testing the concept for over a year, Manufacturers Hanover Trust dropped it because of problems with operational controls. However, the concept was picked up and further improved upon by Citibank, which reported a 75 percent drop in fraud after the first year. In the early 1970s, following the success of Citibank and others, a number of banks began the process of using post-mailers in combination with dual dating.

Warning bulletins alerting banks and merchants to fraudulent cards were another preventive measure adopted by the banks. Although warning bulletins would appear to have been both a commonsensical and reasonable approach, many in the industry were skeptical of its effectiveness, particularly in light of its great expense. The value of printed hot card lists for merchants had been a controversial subject since the first one was published by Diners Club in 1954 (when first-class postage was only 3¢). Since postage accounted for two-thirds of the cost of warning bulletins, escalating postage costs made it an increasingly expensive alternative. By 1977, the cost of warning bulletins had soared to $12 million per year, and many companies questioned whether they were worthwhile.

American Express, Diners Club, Carte Blanche, and Interbank all felt that the warning bulletins were necessary to control fraud as well as misuse of cards by delinquents and overspenders. Visa, on the other hand, took the position that warning bulletins were not necessary and that postcards sufficed. Statistically, Visa banks were losing a higher percentage of their charge volume from fraud than were Master Charge banks. However, Visa clung to its archaic system throughout the 1970s because it was cheaper than printing and distributing warning bulletins.

Eventually, many individual Visa banks in high-risk areas of the country put out their own warning bulletins. These included Chase Manhattan and Bankers Trust in the New York area and banks in Cleveland, Cincinnati, Baltimore, and Dallas. By the late 1970s, less than 50 percent of Visa banks used the postcard, and some disdained any type of warning system.

Losses due to fraud continued throughout the 1970s. By 1980, fraud loss on credit cards was estimated to be nearly $250 million, or 0.29 percent of the $145 billion charged that year in the United States. Hardest hit by far were the bank cards, whose fraud losses totaled 0.52 percent of sales. Retailers and oil companies had the lowest fraud losses, with 0.12 percent of sales.

In large part, the banks themselves were responsible for their continuing losses due to theft. In their desire to market their cards as actively as possible, they were reluctant to tarnish the image of the credit card by publicizing stories of thefts and losses, so they played down fraud in order to not alarm potential cardholders. In addition, the refusal of BankAmericard and American Express to cooperate with Master Charge, Diners Club, and Carte Blanche on a joint warning bulletin hindered the industry's attempts to limit its fraud losses.

As the 1970s drew to a close, the credit card companies had finally overcome most of the legal and operational problems that had arisen in the wake of their tremendous expansion. A wide array of laws and regulations now governed the operations of credit card companies, providing protection for consumers and stabilizing the industry.

6

The Pursuit of Profitability

SOLVING THEIR LEGAL AND OPERATIONAL difficulties was only a means to an end for the bank card companies, and that end was making a profit. Unlike the retail and gas cards, which were viewed primarily as marketing ventures, the universal cards existed exclusively as money-making propositions. Unfortunately for the bank card companies, despite their enormous growth in all other areas—in cardholders, in sales, in merchant outlets, and in participating banks—they could not seem to achieve growth in the area of profits.

In the first profitability study undertaken by NBI in 1972, 217 BankAmericard programs were examined and a strong correlation was found between the age of the bank's card operation and profitability. No similar relationship was found between profitability and the size of the bank. The key factor in profitability appeared to be the proportion of mature customer accounts held by the bank. A mature account was one with a solid record of timely payments. These findings were neither unexpected nor particularly helpful. Mature accounts could be obtained only by waiting until all of the marginal accounts had washed out. A certain amount of loss had to be absorbed for each mature account gained. Banks could also purchase mature accounts from other banks, but this did not occur much until several years later.

Increasing Revenues

As they struggled to stem losses from their credit card operations, the banks experimented with all of the profit-related variables under their control. Unable to raise finance charges because of restrictive usury ceilings in virtually every state, and unwilling to impose an annual fee for fear of losing customers, they raised merchant discounts until the merchants threatened to desert them, marketed other products to their customers through various "cross-selling" programs, rented out their cardholder lists, sold advertising space on their remittance envelopes, and adjusted their methods of calculating finance charges—all in search of higher revenues.

The biggest disappointment at the start of the decade was the realization that too many cardholders paid their balances promptly. Banks had originally predicted that 70 percent would defer payment, producing 1.5 percent monthly interest on a huge unpaid balance, but they experienced just the reverse: only about 30 percent of cardholders used the card for installment buying. The cost of maintaining accounting records and bearing the float for the vast majority of customers who generated no interest income was a heavy burden.

In some areas of the country, the profitable segment of cardholders was as low as 20 percent, and some analysts predicted that the more sophisticated and higher income customers would never pay 18 percent per year for borrowed money. By 1973, statements were sent to only about 57 percent of both BankAmericard and Master Charge cardholders, indicating widespread inactivity. Furthermore, the average sales slip was only $19.45 for Master Charge and $18.23 for BankAmericard, figures that held little promise for large unpaid balances from which the banks could derive interest income.

The banks' first response was to raise the basic interest rate, but that move was stymied by restrictive usury laws that existed in most states. There was considerable variation in usury laws from state to state. In the mid-1970s, Minnesota had the lowest interest ceiling in the country at 8 percent. Montgomery Ward challenged the applicability of this ceiling to revolving credit, but the generality of the ceiling was sustained by a judge in St. Paul.

Montgomery Ward's experience was indicative of the difficulty the banks had in trying to circumvent usury laws. According to data compiled by Professor Robert W. Johnson of Purdue University's Credit Research Center, at the end of the 1970s, thirty-seven of the fifty states had usury ceilings on credit cards. Only three states had no limit; two had limits that were above 18 percent. Three additional states allowed rates of above 18 percent for a portion of the balance, while the remainder was set at lower rates.

Kept from raising the actual interest rate, the banks began to tinker with a nearly invisible means of increasing revenue: changes in the method of calculating finance charges. Most bank card plans had originally used the "adjusted balance" method (used by many retailers) whereby finance charge were levied only on the total balance unpaid at the time payment was due. In other words, if a credit card customer's payment was due on the sixth of the month and he or she paid off $100 of the $1,000 outstanding balance, interest would be charged only on the $900 unpaid balance and would only accrue from the sixth of that month.

By moving to the "average daily balance" system, the banks assessed a finance charge on a daily basis from the date a charge was made (rather than from the due date for the payment) and did not assess finance charges only if the entire outstanding balance was paid in full by the due date of the payment. In the extreme case, a customer who charged $1,000 in merchandise on the first day of the payment period and repaid all but a penny of that sum on the due date of the payment would be assessed full interest on the $1,000 for the entire month. It was estimated that changing to the average daily balance system could generate between 15 and 25 percent additional credit revenue. By 1 March 1975, when Bank of America finally switched to the average daily balance system, more than two-thirds of bank card issuers had made the change.

Another method the banks employed to increase revenues was marketing other products to their customers, a practice known as cross-selling. Credit card companies have long recognized the value of stuffing their monthly statements with solicitations for other goods and services. The marginal cost is low because postage has already been paid and the customer is prequalified, being both creditworthy and in possession of a vehicle to pay for the product.

This periodic contact with the customer has long been seen by retailers as one of the major benefits of offering a private-label credit card. Both retailers and oil companies have used "stuffers" to promote the sale of their other products for several decades. But these programs were never very successful for the universal cards. Part of the problem was that the credit card companies had few if any of their own products to market. The banks also had to overcome the strong identification of the card with the bank card company (either Master Charge or Bank-Americard), not with the issuing bank. Since customers identified the card with the bank card company rather than the bank, the bank was discouraged from promoting its other products through stuffers. The identification problem was compounded by the practice of mailing bills from the bank card company rather than from the bank. Finally, a substantial cross-selling problem was the fact that by its very nature the bank card process did not motivate the customer to physically visit the bank, where other products could be sold.

In an attempt to improve their cross-selling ability, a number of banks in the early 1970s began packaging the credit card with several other bank services into a single service for which a fee was charged. One of the first of these was the Wells Fargo Gold Account program. Begun 5 February 1973, Wells Fargo charged $36 per year for a program that included a check-cashing identification card, unlimited free checkingt, free personalized checks, a safe-deposit box, free traveler's checks, cashier's checks, and money orders, a Master Charge card, overdraft protection (using the credit line on the Master Charge card), and reduced interest rates on personal loans. The program was successful from its inception, bringing in more than 12,000 applications by the end of the second week.

By the end of 1973, Wells Fargo could report an unqualified success with its Gold Account card. In contrast to its first-year projection of 50,000 requests for the card, it received 84,277 Gold Account requests within just six months, and 18 percent were from new bank customers. The concept won Wells Fargo the top trophy in the marketing category of the Bank Marketing Association. Perhaps more indicative of its success, by the end of 1973, more than 300 banks across the country were offering similar packages, and Wells Fargo had so many inquiries about the Gold Account program that it was forced to hold seminars to explain the program to prospective users.

Because of the limited number of their own products they could sell through their mailings, bank card companies began to promote the sale of other products. This practice had been first tried by Diners Club in 1956 when it began marketing an insurance plan to cardholders. The first fifteen years of the program produced a net of nearly $5.5 million. Most of the major oil companies also offered insurance to their cardholders, often through a travel club.

An example of the type of cross-selling program available to banks was a plan begun on 1 January 1973 to merchandise Longines mail-order products through the bank card industry. The program was headed by Joe Cirillo of the Cooper-Rand Corporation, which conducted a coordinated series of monthly promotions tailored to the demographics of each bank's customers. The products being promoted included fire extinguishers, cookware, tape recorders, coin collections, calculators, radios, and photographs reproduced on canvas. The bank received a 15 percent commission for its participation.

One of the most innovative attempts to cross-sell other products was the Gold Key Auto charge card, which gave holders preapproved credit sufficient to purchase an automobile. The card was first marketed by Motivational Systems Inc. in 1973, and the Walker Bank and Trust Company in Salt Lake City was the first bank to take part in the program. In the first thirteen months of operation, Walker Bank and Trust signed up 197 dealers, of whom 166 had made at least one sale. Walker Bank and Trust was able to increase its automobile loan portfolio by 165 percent.

Another means of earning additional income has been through the use of advertising on remittance envelopes in monthly statements. The idea of using remittance envelopes as an advertising medium was first tested in 1957 with a number of department stores by National Envelope Advertising Company. The sales pitch is that credit card companies get their envelopes free. In addition to this savings, the credit card companies are given a percentage of the sales generated by the advertising on the envelopes.

The following example illustrates the revenue potential of this plan. First, the credit card company receives envelopes for free, which saves it $5 per 1,000 envelopes. Second, it is estimated that the average bank will receive twenty orders per 1,000 envelopes mailed, or a 2 percent return. On a typical order of $10, this return rate would produce $200 in gross sales, and with a 20 percent commission, the profit would be $40 plus the $5 saving on the envelopes—or $45 for each 1,000 statements mailed. Therefore, a bank with 100,000 customers would mail 1.2 million statements in a year and would realize 1,200 × $45, or $54,000 per year in additional net income.

In the late 1970s, another dimension was added to credit card sales promotion by the introduction of In-Wats companies to accept toll-free orders. The value of In-Wats was to make offers whose appeal was more spontaneous than that of offers by mailer. By 1980, nearly 5 percent of credit card orders came over the telephone.

Despite all of these attempts, profitability continued to be a chimera for many bank card companies throughout the 1970s. Although Federal Reserve functional cost analysis data from the period indicates that the net pretax margins on bank credit card debt were positive from 1972 to 1979, the return was significantly below that on other types of bank debt. Many banks actually lost money on their credit card operations during this period, as did the industry as a whole in the inflationary period from 1979 to 1981 when the rising cost of funds forced many credit card companies into the red.

Although the banks had been willing to absorb losses during the early growth years of the industry, by the late 1970s they could no longer carry their poorly performing credit card operations. The Regulation Q phaseout, which was completed in 1976, eliminated the ceilings on interest rates banks could pay deposits, thereby ending the "easy" profits banks could earn on the spreads between deposits and loans. Banks could no longer afford to carry losses on their credit card operations, and each service would have to start paying for itself. Bank cards would have to be revenue producers in the present, not just long-term investments. Banks had to increase rates and service charges wherever possible to compete more effectively for the "profitable" customer who would run up large amounts of unpaid debt on his or her credit card.

Annual Fees

One constant problem that the banks had been unable to address were the "free riders," the sizable proportion of bank card users who did not revolve their balances and who deprived the bank of finance charge income. Solving this problem was the key to achieving profitability, but the solution was one that the banks were not willing to employ—imposing an annual fee.

During the late 1970s, as rising interest rates drove up the cost of money, more and more banks looked to the annual fee as the only way to make their credit card operations profitable. Prior to this time, there had been only a few attempts at imposing an annual fee, with mixed results. The first bank in the United States to charge an annual membership fee for its charge card was the Marquette Bank of Minnesota. When the $10 membership fee went into effect in 1973, the bank had approximately 100,000 BankAmericard accounts. As a result of the 12 percent state usury ceiling, which the Minnesota legislature refused to lift, Marquette estimated that it had accumulated $1.8 million in pretax losses on its BankAmericard division since 1968.

One of the key selling points used by Marquette to market the fee was that the $10 fee was less than the finance charges that most bank cardholders ran up in the course of a year on "free" cards. Marquette correctly estimated that 30–40 percent of its cardholder base would drop out when fees were imposed; subsequent analysis showed that most of the dropouts were inactive. Although this was a successful move for Marquette, it was not emulated by other banks at that time. Marquette had been faced with the situation of charging a fee or getting out of the business. In other states where the usury ceiling was much higher, there was not as much incentive to impose an annual fee. Any bank that did so unilaterally was likely to lose customers to its competitors.

In 1976, Citibank shocked the credit card industry with its decision to charge any Master Charge cardholder who paid up within the interest-free period 50¢ per month. Although Citibank and Marquette were attempting to solve the same problem, the unfortunate structure of Citibank's program sparked a fire of negative publicity. The reaction to Citibank's attempt to stem some $98 million in losses over seven years was almost universally critical. Thomas R. Wilcox, chairman of Crocker National Bank, made a direct attack on Citibank's 50¢ plan, calling it a "strategic error." Crocker considered its Master Charge operation a "loss leader," and Wilcox said that Citibank's error was in trying to make its credit card operation a profit center. Wilcox also observed that Citibank was "not adroit" in the way that it handled the announcement.

Even Congress joined the denunciations. In a joint statement, Democratic Congressman Frank Annunzio of Illinois and Democratic Congressman Walter Fauntroy of Washington, D.C. stated that Citibank had trapped consumer credit card users by initiating the monthly service charge and that they would ask Congress to outlaw the practice.

Citibank's defense was that its 50¢ monthly charge would cost cardholders at most only $6 per year, compared with the $20 fee for T&E cards. Unfortunately, its customers did not find this a compelling argument. In a period of slightly more than two months, from May through 15 July 1976, Citibank experienced more than 7,000 cancellations. In the spring of 1978, the Citibank 50¢ card fee was ruled illegal in a decision by the Supreme Court of the State of New York, and Citibank discontinued it. According to Citibank, the period during which the fee had been in effect was the only time it had made money on its credit card operation.

The primary legal question about the annual fee was whether it constituted a membership fee or another form of finance charge. Up until the late 1970s, the only legal precedent for the imposition of an annual fee was a 1971 Federal Reserve interpretation of Regulation Z, the truth-in-lending law. At that time, the Fed, declaring the fee to be a "qualification of membership and for issuance of the card," apparently regarded it as a finance charge.

In 1976, the innovative Worthen Bank, which had pioneered bank card duality, sought to resolve this issue through the courts. Feeling that its profits were hindered by the 10 percent interest ceiling in Arkansas, the bank initiated a test case by charging a single customer, Mrs. Donna

Key, a token $12 annual fee for the use of Master Charge and BankAmericard services. Worthen's efforts were rewarded when Arkansas Supreme Court Justice Elsijane Roy ruled that such a fee was "not a cloak for usury" but constituted payment for valued services available to all bank cardholders.

Although Worthen did not generally charge an annual fee for its bank cards at the time of the ruling, the Arkansas Supreme Court allowed it to do so when it wanted. Following this action, Worthen decided to charge a $15 annual fee for dual-issued Visa and Master Charge cards, or $12 for either one alone.

Aside from the legal difficulties in some states, banks were reluctant to impose annual fees because of the highly competitive nature of the bank card system at the bank level. Since bank cards were free to consumers and even the rate they paid on credit balances was determined by the state, any bank that unilaterally began to charge a fee for bank card membership would be likely to lose a large proportion of its customers to other banks that did not charge such a fee. There were other isolated attempts to institute annual fees besides Marquette's and Worthen's. In Connecticut, for example, most of the state's largest commercial banks initiated a $5 fee in 1977 following a survey by the Banking Center of Waterbury that revealed that consumers would accept up to a $10 fee. But that was by far the exception to the rule. What banks clearly needed was some type of legal action that would compel them to institute a fee simultaneously.

On 14 March 1980, President Jimmy Carter announced a number of new policy initiatives to help curb inflation. One of these policies was directed specifically at credit cards and other types of unsecured consumer credit. The new policy required that creditors with more than $2 million in consumer credit outstanding establish special deposits with the Federal Reserve into which they would place 15 percent of all unsecured credit expended after 14 March 1980. These accounts would be noninterest-bearing and would constitute, in effect, a penalty for those creditors that expanded their total outstanding consumer credit.

According to the Federal Reserve Board, which was responsible for enforcing this policy, the special deposit requirement was designed to encourage restraint on such credit extensions. It said that specific methods used by banks to achieve this restraint were up to the individual firms. As a result of this policy, banks, which were already losing substantial amounts of money on their credit card operations, had even less incentive to add to their totals outstanding.

This was the opportunity the banks needed. A short time after the enactment of credit controls, a substantial number of banks announced the imposition of annual fees. The Society National Bank of Cleveland announced a $20 annual fee, Bank Ohio a $12 fee, First American of Nashville an $18 fee, and Iowa Des Moines National Bank a $15 fee. In addition, another large group of banks announced that interest rates would be increased. A number of banks initially held back to see what the consumer reaction would be. In her analysis of the situation, Joyce Healy, vice president of Manufacturers Hanover Trust of New York, said that emergency measures provided a rare opportunity for the banking industry to adjust prices to decide who their important customers were.

Within several months after the fees were imposed, it was clear that they did not result in the large anticipated loses in cardholder base. In California, Security Pacific's $15 fee cost it 8 percent of its one million accounts. Bank of America's $12 fee resulted in a 6 percent cancellation rate, and Crocker's combination of a 12¢ transaction fee and an interest rate increase from 18 to 21 percent resulted in less than a one percent loss. In New York, all of the larger banks, with the exception of Bank of New York and European-American, added fees.

The imposition of fees marked the end of the expansive phase of bank credit cards. In response to the annual fees, cardholders surrendered over nine million bank cards in 1980, amounting to some 8 percent of the total. The loss of a substantial number of cardholders had the greatest negative impact on the smaller merchants who lacked alternative means of credit. But it had a positive impact on the nationwide retailers, who could retain and further promote their own "free" cards at the expense of the bank cards.

Growth and Profits

The combination of annual fees and the dramatic drop in interest rates in the 1980s allowed the banks to achieve, after many years of losses and marginal gains, a high level of profitability in their credit card operations. After having trailed all other bank operations for most of the 1970s and early 1980s, by 1984 bank credit card operations were outperforming all other forms of bank debt. Since 1984, their pretax margins have exceeded those on real estate, installment, and commercial debt. From 1984 to 1986, credit card returns averaged 3.6 percent, while the returns on other forms of bank debt were 2.4 percent on mortgages, 2.7 percent on consumer installment debt, and 1.4 percent on commercial and other loans.

The 1980s marked the close of the expansive phase of the credit card industry and the establishment of a mature marketplace. Fueled by increasing profits and the elimination of most legal and operational difficulties, the bank card industry entered a tremendous period of growth from the early 1980s through the decade.

Several factors contributed to the growth spurt. During the so-called "Carter inflation," the interest cost of funds rose into the high teens, causing banks to lose money on their credit card outstandings. As a result, many states raised usury ceilings to allow the banks a positive spread. In fact, there were seventeen states that had no limit on credit card rates or fees in 1988.

When rates fell during the mid-1980s, a few banks lowered their rates to attract more business, but most concluded that the segment that revolves credit is not particularly rate-sensitive. Consequently, most credit card rates remained in the high teens, producing large profits for the banks. A number of banks also took advantage of consumer complaisance by changing annual fees, rates, grace periods, late charges, and other card restrictions without attracting a great deal of consumer attention.

Other factors contributing to the credit card industry boom were the tremendous growth in consumer credit and, more significantly, the growing importance of the credit card as a vehicle for consumer debt. A study by Glenn Canner on the credit card industry from 1970 to 1986 revealed that, although the proportion of credit card owners who used the revolving credit feature remained nearly constant during this period at about 50 percent, the average outstanding balance more than doubled in real terms—from $649 in 1970 to $1,472 in 1986. Much of the growth in consumer debt came in the early and mid-1980s. In 1983, consumer credit card debt accounted for 16.9 percent of total installment payments. By 1986, it had increased to 25.3 percent of payments. This increase coincided with the surge in the proportion of consumer debt to disposable personal income, from 14 percent in 1982 to 18 percent in 1986.

The growth of the credit card industry during this period received additional impetus from the increased participation of banks. Recognizing the tremendous profits that were being reaped, many banks that had previously eschewed a credit card program promptly jumped on the bandwagon. In 1979, only 71 percent of banks offered MasterCard or Visa. By 1985, 90 percent of all banks offered a Visa and 87 percent a MasterCard. By the end of 1986, banks held nearly two-thirds of total credit card outstanding balances, up from one-half in 1982. Credit card receivables had become 5 percent of total bank loans by 1986, up from 3 percent in 1982.

Affinity Cards

By the mid-1980s, the credit card market had reached its saturation point and credit card companies were faced with an increasingly competitive market for new customers. Most consumers already carried an average of three credit cards; the companies needed to develop new marketing techniques to persuade consumers to change or add cards to their already bulging wallets. One of the most popular, and initially one of the most successful, marketing programs of the 1980s was the affinity card. Affinity cards were begun in 1985 when MasterCard and Visa first allowed the names of organizations other than banks to appear on their cards. Within a year, there were 296 affinity programs. By 1988, an estimated twenty-six million cardholders carried 2,725 different affinity cards—each with its own distinctive look—and the number grew by 872 in the first six months of 1988.

Affinity card programs have been developed for an incredibly wide range of special interest groups, from First Interstate Bank of California's Visa card for North American sheep supporters to the card promoted jointly by Breyer's Ice Cream and Marine Midland Bank in New York. Generally, the cards fall into three categories: product benefit cards, lifestyle cards, and personality cards. Product benefit cards provide the user with a finite benefit, such as frequent-flier bonus miles for every dollar spent. Lifestyle cards are sponsored by groups with a common bond, often a charitable cause: a card issued by Commercial Federal in Omaha benefits local Catholic schools, and one issued by Empire of America Federal Savings Bank benefits AIDS research. Some cards are distributed by charitable organizations that are paid by the issuing banks for the success of their card programs. Personality cards focus on specific personalities such as the Elvis Presley card marketed by Leader Federal Bank for Savings in Memphis, or the New York Giants card issued by First Fidelity Bank in Newark, New Jersey.

Banks found affinity card programs attractive for two reasons. First, as the market reached its saturation point for regular bank cards, a new motivation was needed to induce the consumer to take on an additional card or to switch from an existing bank card. Second, by targeting groups with known financial attributes, credit risk could be reduced and/ or volume increased. For example, Citibank's frequent-flier program, which is affiliated with American Airlines, has 200,000 cardholders whose average income is $75,000. On average, they use their cards fourteen times each month; the average cardholder uses his or her card only eleven times per month.

By marketing a card that serves a charity, the banks can add a profitable segment to their customer base. A study cited in the 11 November 1988 issue of *Advertising Age* reported that 45 percent of consumers who hold both an affinity and a traditional credit card use the affinity card more often. A second study, conducted by Visa in June 1988, revealed that affinity card solicitations produced two to three times the number of applications for cards as did solicitations for regular cards. The Visa study also indicated that affinity cardholders tend to spend more on their cards, and that for 44 percent of them the affinity card is the first Visa card that they have ever held.

A glut of affinity card offerings in recent years has dimmed their marketing appeal. Recent studies by *American Banker* and others have shown that the "affinity" aspect of the card is less important to most users than the special terms offered, such as reduced interest rates or annual fees, worldwide travel insurance for trips charged on the card, and discounts on travel and hotel accommodations.

Further militating against the continued proliferation of affinity cards is their cost. Frequent-flier programs may cost banks as much as 2¢ per mile. The sponsors of affinity cards, such as charitable organizations, also drive a hard bargain at the outset of the relationship, or at renewal, often demanding the entire first-year fee as well as a percentage of the sales volume generated by the card. Because of increasingly intense competition for cardholders, banks have been forced to offer better and better terms to the affinity groups, eliminating much of the profitability from affinity cards. Although many affinity programs continue to be profitable ventures, many banks, such as Chemical Bank in New York, have decided to drop them entirely.

Secured Cards and Prestige Cards

Credit card companies have also intensified their marketing efforts toward both the high and the low end of the market. On the low end, they have sought to increase their cardholder base by developing programs for consumers who would not qualify for a regular credit card. The most successful program of this type has been the "secured" credit card. After obtaining deposits from customers with poor credit histories or low incomes, several banks have issued them cards with credit lines equal to the amount of money they have deposited. In this way, the banks have "secured" the credit card and protected themselves from any losses due to payment failure.

A few banks have specialized in providing secured credit cards to the high-risk market. Key Federal Savings and Loan in Maryland has operated a secured card program since 1982. By 1988, it had more than 50,000 such accounts with $28 million in outstanding debts, which were collateralized by $29 million in deposits.

A number of nonbank firms have also entered the secured card market, acting as intermediaries between high-risk individuals and the credit card companies. As of 1988, nearly fifteen million Americans have tried but were unable to obtain a credit card, and each year more than 2.6 million more are added to this pool, creating a tremendous market for the nonbank intermediaries. In 1988, an estimated 1.125 million Americans who could not qualify for an unsecured bank card paid more than $50 million to brokers of secured cards. According to the *Nilson Report*, only about 10 percent of these applicants ended up with a credit card.

A much more lucrative and more intense battle has been waged at the high end of the market. Before 1981, the "prestige" card field had been dominated by American Express, Diners Club, and Carte Blanche. Aside from the prestige accorded by an upscale card, its primary benefit was the much larger line of credit, which was important to business travelers and those who entertained a great deal.

Recognizing the potential of the prestige card market, MasterCard introduced its gold card in June 1981; Visa quickly followed suit, launching its Premier card in 1982. Their primary competitors were American Express, which controlled the vast majority of the market, followed by Carte Blanche and Diners Club, both of which by then were owned by Citibank. By 1987, the bank card companies had secured a combined total of more than thirteen million cardholders. By 1988, Visa Gold (the Premier card's new name) and MasterCard Gold accounted for more than 37 percent of the upscale market, and the *Nilson Report* predicted that these totals would reach 54 percent by 1990, and 69 percent by 1995.

Despite their tremendous growth, Visa Gold and MasterCard Gold still trail American Express. As of 1988, the American Express green card was the most widely held and used prestige card in the world, accounting for more than 40 percent of the U.S. market share in cards and 41.4 percent in volume—followed by MasterCard Gold, Amex Gold, and more distantly, Diners Club and Carte Blanche. Visa Gold and MasterCard Gold, however, continue to represent a major challenge to American Express. In 1988, their annual fees averaged just under $40, slightly less than the $45 charged by American Express for its green card and significantly less than the $65 charged for its gold card. More importantly, the bank cards were accepted at 2.5 million merchant locations in the United States and at 5.9 million worldwide, as opposed to 1.4 million locations for Amercian Express in the United States and 2.1 million worldwide—a marked advantage and selling point for the bank cards.

In response to the encroachment by the bank cards on a market it had previously held complete control over, American Express launched the Optima card in 1987. The Optima card created a considerable amount of concern among bankers. Unlike its green card, which has no revolving credit feature, and its gold card, which has revolving credit provided by a participating bank, the Optima card is strictly a revolving credit card, with credit provided by American Express.

By mid-1988, American Express had mailed Optima cards to nearly 1.5 million American Express cardholders and had produced over $1 billion in revolving balances at the Centurion Bank, which is an American Express subsidiary in Delaware. The advantages of paying an additional $15 for the Optima card included acceptance at all locations that already accepted other American Express cards, a low variable rate of interest tied to the prime rate reported in the *Wall Street Journal* (13.55 percent in 1987), and a separate statement for Optima charges.

Research conducted by American Express indicated that a large number of green card users desired a revolving credit option for some purposes but wanted the monthly payoff discipline imposed by the green card for others. However, bankers worried that the low-interest Optima card would attract Amex Gold cardholders, whose revolving balances were held by the banks, as well as Visa and MasterCard users, who would no longer need a bank card for revolving credit.

Visa mounted a campaign to remind bankers of the threat posed by American Express and its Optima card. The bank card companies judged the new card to have a good chance of success. American Express had no marketing expense for signing up merchants who already accepted its other cards, and little marketing expense for getting Optima into the hands of its own cardholders. Furthermore, by offering the card only to its best credit risks, American Express minimized its loss exposure and collection costs.

The next step for American Express appears to be a marketing campaign to customers who do not have an American Express card of any type. Visa and MasterCard will undoubtedly be spurred to counter this attack on their market—a not so surprising turnabout considering their foray into American Express's domain earlier in the decade.

The Discover Card

American Express's Optima card is not the only new competitor to challenge Visa and MasterCard. In April 1986, one year before the introduction of the Optima card, Sears surprised the credit card industry with the introduction of its Discover card. Designed as a universal card that would compete with Visa and MasterCard, Discover was issued by Greenwood Trust Company, a Delaware-based bank owned by Sears.

At the time Discover was launched, Sears was at a crossroad. Its retail business had been slipping for many years, and the company had been moving into the financial services business with the acquisition of the Dean Witter brokerage company and the Caldwell Banker real estate company to complement its Allstate insurance subsidiary. The Discover card was seen as another financial service that would allow Sears to diversify itself from its retail operation.

Unfortunately for Sears, by 1986 bank card profitability was near its all-time high and the market was close to its saturation point. To make its new card attractive to customers, Sears did not charge an annual fee and even gave a rebate to users based on volume. The rebate could be used to reduce account balances and to buy merchandise in Sears stores, or it could be deposited to a Discover savings account at Greenwood Trust Company. Sears sought to offset these benefits with an interest rate of 19.8 percent, among the highest in the industry.

In its first year of operation, Sears lost $106 million on the Discover card but succeeded in getting it into the hands of some thirteen million people, as well as accepted by 550,000 merchants. By the end of the second year, its cardholder base had grown to twenty-two million, but losses increased to $124 million. Discover's two problems were merchant acceptance and cardholder use. Many merchants, fearing retail competition from Sears, were loathe to take the Discover card. In addition, studies showed that charges and revolving balances were just over half those generated on Visa and MasterCard. Since consumers paid nothing for the card, many obviously acquired one with no serious intention to use it.

Discover earned its first profit, $6.4 million, in the first quarter of 1988, but its profit sank to just $100,000 in the second quarter. And despite steady growth in the number of both cardholders and participating merchants, Discover continues to trail the two bank cards by a considerable margin. In 1988, only 25 percent of all consumers carried a Discover card, as opposed to 70 percent who carried Visa and MasterCard. Similarly, only 30 to 40 percent of merchants accepted the Discover card; 98 percent accepted Visa and MasterCard.

In October 1988, Sears began two marketing tests of its credit cards. Selected stores began accepting Visa, MasterCard, and American Express cards in addition to the Sears and Discover cards. In addition, Sears began charging Discover cardholders in North Carolina and Wisconsin an annual fee of $15. Sears faces some difficult choices about the

Discover card. Like the bank cards, it cannot become very profitable without an annual fee. However, once a fee is charged, Sears risks substantial defections from users who have a bank card that is accepted in 98 percent of merchant locations, rather than 30 to 40 percent.

Telephone Charge Cards

While contending with these challenges to their traditional market, the bank card companies continue to branch out into new markets. The latest target is the telephone charge card market, worth $5 billion per year. Although AT&T currently dominates this market, with nearly 60 percent of the seventy-five million cards in circulation, in 1989 Visa entered into an agreement with MCI Communications that would enable MCI's customers to charge their calls directly to their Visa card, thereby eliminating the need for an MCI card. Called VisaPhone, the service is being tested at forty banks across the country. Eventually, more than 20,000 banks are expected to participate. Visa is also negotiating similar agreements with U.S. Sprint and AT&T.

The arrangement is beneficial to both MCI and Visa. The plan gives MCI access to 120 million Visa cards in circulation. Moreover, their owners all fit the demographic model for MCI customers, who travel a lot, spend a lot, are better educated, have a higher income, and like to use ATMs. That fit translates into increased usage and sales for MCI. For Visa, the program appears equally advantageous. Having saturated most major markets, Visaphone gives it a rare opportunity to expand into a completely new market.

Visa is not the first credit card company to enter the telephone charge card market, however. American Express had already entered into such an agreement with MCI, allowing MCI customers to charge their calls to their American Express card. However, unlike Visa cardholders, who can use their Visa account number as their MCI called card number, American Express cardholders still have to use their MCI account numbers to place calls.

Competition Overseas—Brazil

Credit companies have also continued to battle for customers in other markets around the world. The competition has been particularly fierce in those markets that have shown considerable growth potential. In Brazil, hyperinflation has triggered a boom in credit card use as consumers seek out ways to escape price increases. (The annual inflation rate for 1988 was over 1,000 percent). The number of credit cards in circulation in Brazil has grown from 3.6 million in 1988 to 6.2 million in 1989, and marketing directors predict that this figure will quintuple by 1993.

All of the major card companies have scrambled to exploit this growth. MasterCard, which is affiliated with Credicard—Brazil's most popular card with 2.2 million users—doubled its cardholder base from 1987 to 1989. During that same period, American Express's cardholder base has grown to 480,000, a 30 percent increase, and the formerly moribund Diners Club franchise has watched its cardholder base triple to more than 300,000.

Visa was one of the last to jump on the bandwagon. But only a year after affiliating itself with Banco de Brasil and Banco Nacional, two of the country's largest commercial banks, it had signed up more than one million customers and is rapidly pushing toward control of the market. Visa is also betting on the eventual easing of government restrictions on credit card use abroad.

Besides hyperinflation, two other factors have fueled the growth of credit card use in Brazil. The first is the changing perception of the credit card: once simply a buying tool, it has now become a social necessity. To appear prosperous and professional, it is essesntial to carry a credit card. The second factor is the change in banking practices with the introduction of EFT systems, primarily ATMs. For the present time, marketing directors look at Brazil as one of the best growth markets in the world. Other observers predict that the current credit card binge will only worsen the country's already serious inflation problems.

Cutting Costs

Increased competition and decreased profitability in the late 1980s have forced banks to look critically at their back room processing operations. Credit card issuers can handle processing themselves, or they can contract with a third-party processor, either for-profit or nonprofit, such as a bank card association.

The decision is often not a simple one. On the one hand, third-party processing is often less expensive than in-house processing, particularly for smaller bank card programs. On the other hand, most banks want to strengthen the relationship with their customers. Integrating credit card data with other customer information enables the bank to service the customer as a complete entity rather than as merely the recipient of various products. Such integration allows, for example, the use of expert systems for customer authorization. While a third party might turn down an over-limit credit card customer, the bank might note substantial balances in checking or savings accounts, an indication that a credit line extension is justified. The best known and most sucessful expert system in the credit card field is American Express's authorizer assistant system, which helps agents decide when to authorize over-limit transactions.

However, software difficulties have caused many banks to opt for third-party processing. There are five primary functions of a credit card processing system: applications and solicitations, credit authorization, accounting for cardholders, collections processing, and merchant processing. Software that will do all five functions is not widely available, and banks have had to do custom programming instead. Keeping software current is a major job, particularly for a bank that is not large enough to have a dedicated team of programmers.

By 1988, there were very few nonprofit, third-party bank card processors, and these were under constant pressure from the better financed and more flexible for-profit companies. To meet the needs of their clients, bank card processors were investing huge amounts of capital in advanced services, including customer databases, information management systems, and customer segmentation procedures, as well as in the ongoing changes mandated by both state and federal regulations and Visa and MasterCard. The nonprofit companies found it hard to keep up, and in the spring of 1988, First Data Resources, the largest nonprofit credit card processor in the world, acquired Eastern States Bank Card Association, the second-largest.

Increased competition among third-party processors has made it possible for many smaller credit card operations to stay in business by contracting out their back room work. Banks that are large enough to maintain their own credit card operations are under pressure to cut costs without sacrificing quality. A number have accomplished this by moving their credit card operations to states with lower labor costs, such as Citibank's move to South Dakota. Some have even been looking into the possibility of locating overseas, preferably in English-speaking countries, such as Ireland.

Securitization

A major source of new revenue for the banks has been securitization. Originally developed for mortgages and installment loans, securitization spread to the credit industry in 1986. Securitization involves the bundling and sale of credit card receivables to investors in the form of securities. The pool of loans is put into a special subsidiary or trust used to back a certificate or note. Investors then buy the certificates or shares in the trust and receive interest and principal payments as the loans are repaid.

Securitization was first introduced for home mortgages. Salomon Brothers, a major New York investment bank, pioneered their use in 1980. In 1985, asset-based securities involving leasing equipment were issued by Sperry Lease, and shortly thereafter, New York's Marine Midland Bank and Arizona's Valley National Bank executed the first public offerings of securities backed by auto loans. In April 1986, Bank One in Ohio introduced the first securities backed by credit card receivables by issuing $50 million in CARDs (certificates for amortizing revolving debts), a name trademarked by Salomon Brothers. The following year, more than $2 billion in credit card securities was issued.

What was the advantage of these securities to the credit card industry? Asset-based securities are turned into liquid, fixed-rate, investment-grade debt, which pays only half a point to a point more than a risk-free Treasury obligation of the same maturity. In this way, the banks can lock in a high finance charge to their customers, paying perhaps only half that amount for the funds that they use.

However, to assure investors that they will not sustain losses from that part of the pool that fails to repay its credit card debt, certain credit enhancements are used. These enhancements are generally sufficient to obtain one of the two highest ratings available from the debt rating agencies, such as Standard and Poor. Enhancements may involve reserve funds held against possible loss, letters of credit from a bank or insurance company, or overcollateralization that pledges more receivables than are needed for the issue. Because of credit enhancements, Bank of America, which had a low debt rating of BBB in 1987, was able to sell credit card securities at AAA interest rates, just approximately three-quarters of a percentage point above comparable Treasury rates.

To synchronize scheduled payments of principal to investors with payment by cardholders, banks are generally given the flexibility of substituting new receivables to replenish the pool of assets in the event of early payoff of debt by cardholders. From the standpoint of the investment marketplace, the relatively short maturity of the instruments secured by credit card receivables makes them particularly attractive. They also lack the great unknown variable that makes mortgage-backed securities so risky—accelerated prepayment, which occurs whenever rates fall.

An alternative to securitization has been the outright sale of credit card portfolios. In the late 1980s, competition combined with lowered interest rates resulted in companies paying premiums of as much as 20 percent of outstanding debt for high-quality portfolios. Portfolios of lower quality were more difficult to securitize but were often sold at discounts that were less than the expected charge-offs.

Increased competition from all sides—Discover, Optima, affinity cards—has begun to erode the profitability of bank card operations. In an effort to meet marketing goals, many banks have taken on customers with lower and lower credit ratings. Dependence upon more marginal accounts with higher balances has resulted in a substantial increase in net charge-offs.

As a percentage of credit card balances, charge-offs in the United States have doubled from 1.5 percent in 1984 to 3.2 percent in 1986. Worldwide, the *Nilson Report* estimated MasterCard and Visa charge-offs to have been 4.01 percent in 1987. In a sample of 148 large banking organizations carried out by the Federal Reserve Bank of Cleveland in 1987, the percentage of charge-offs ranged from 0.6 to 8.9 percent. Banks with higher charge-off ratios tended to be much larger than others, put more emphasis on credit card lending, and had higher rates. The higher rates tended to compensate the banks for the greater risk of their portfolios.

Charge-offs were primarily attributable to credit problems rather than fraud, which accounted for only about 16 percent of U.S. losses in 1987. The *Nilson Report* estimates that 56.6 percent of credit losses were for nonpayment, 36.6 percent were for bankruptcy, and 6.8 percent resulted from the death of the cardholder. The major type of fraud in 1987 was stolen cards, with 26.6 percent, followed by lost cards and fraudulent applications, with 19.1 percent and 17.7 percent of fraud losses, respectively. As of 1989, the seven-year expansion in the economy had kept recession-induced charge-offs at bay. However, the possibility for major charge-offs exists in the event of a major economic downturn.

Looking to the Future

Today, credit cards have become a major profit center for many banks, but there are numerous warning signs on the horizon. With the industry having peaked in 1984 and many consumers being fully extended, banks have struggled to maintain earlier profit levels. The unprecedented period in the 1980s of economic expansion without a downturn caused banks to lower credit extensions beyond limits formerly considered prudent, and profits have been obtained at the risk of severe charge-offs in the event of a downturn.

Efforts to wring profits from other bank operations have also threatened to erode credit card returns. It is a widely recognized fact that consumers with surplus equity in a home (generally, more than 25 percent of the outstanding mortgage) are better credit risks than those who either do not own a home or have not accumulated equity above a standard down payment. As the banks continue to market home equity loans, they erode the best market for their credit card portfolios—those who revolve credit but pay on time. A few banks have even established a credit card that accesses home equity credit, but the practice has not spread because of its inherent complexity, as well as the fear of the larger banks that, if highly publicized, such cards might result in restrictive legislation, since they are not in keeping with the spirit of the Tax Reform Act of 1986.

Several legislative initiatives have in fact threatened the continued strength of the bank card industry. Many banks fear that the Tax Reform Act's phaseout on interest deductions that are not secured with home equity will eventually slow the use of the credit card as a vehicle for consumer debt. Total phaseout was initially planned for 1991, but legislation introduced in 1989 threatened to move that deadline up a year.

Consumer groups and advocates have also begun to complain about the huge spread between the banks' cost of funds and the interest rates assessed on the cards. They have urged Congress to set national usury ceilings. Through the efforts of the powerful banking lobby, this movement has been partially slowed, resulting in a compromise bill—the Fair Credit and Charge Card Disclosure Act of 1988. Rather than regulate rates, the act concentrates on adequate disclosure of rates and fees to consumers. It mandates conspicuous disclosure of all basic costs at least thirty days prior to annual card renewal. It also regulates solicitations for new accounts by requiring similar disclosure, and it prohibits the marketing of attractive provisions without revealing all costs and fees.

Other possible legislation that would restrict card profitability includes proposals for risk-based capital standards for the banks. To avoid a repeat of massive failures such as happened in the savings and loan industry—brought on in part by risky investment behavior because depositors were protected by the FDIC—regulators have proposed that banks maintain capital against off–balance sheet risks such as unused lines of credit on credit cards. The theory is that, in a recession, consumers who are strapped for funds might use the untapped credit in their lines, thus increasing the exposure of the banks without allowing the banks any control. Since, on average, consumers tend to use only about half of their credit lines, such exposure would be considerable. One advantage of securitization is that it gets existing receivables off the balance sheet, thereby reducing capital requirements for the bank.

Emboldened by surging profits and rising numbers of cardholders, and riding on the shoulders of a seven-year bull market, many banks have come to rely heavily upon the profits generated by their credit card operations. However, as increased competition both from other banks and from new rivals such as Discover and Optima has eroded profits, the banks are once more struggling to keep their credit card operations profitable.

7

Retail and Oil Cards

DESPITE THE TREMENDOUS GROWTH OF the bank cards in the 1970s, the nonfinancial cards—retail and oil—continued to operate sizable operations into the 1980s. The retail cards and, to a lesser extent, the oil company cards maintained their market share despite the persistent efforts of the bank card companies to make inroads into the nonfinancial credit card markets. In fact, while the bank card companies surpassed all other credit cards in the amount of annual billings, the retailers continued to maintain an edge in the number of cardholders. As of 1988, the top four card issuers in the United States were all retailers, led by Sears.

A major problem for the bank card companies, and a key defense for the retailers and oil companies, was access. Although the bank card companies had gained access to the gas industry in the 1960s, various political upheavals in the 1970s allowed the oil companies to refuse bank cards for long periods. And despite being accepted by the smaller merchants for most of the 1970s, bank cards were not honored at any of the larger retail chains until the end of the decade. Even then, the banks quickly discovered that access did not guarantee success.

The bank card companies' lack of success in gaining entrance to these markets could be traced to a fundamental difference between third-party and store-specific credit cards. Considered a marketing tool and a vehicle for extending credit to charge account customers, the retail card was never burdened with the pressure of producing profits. There was no need, as there was with the third-party cards, to expand continually and pursue new methods of increasing revenues. Consequently, retail cards did not have the same enormous marketing costs as the bank cards did, and retailers' collection costs and losses due to fraud on their cards were minimal. Retailers were not forced, as were the bank card companies, to accept customers who they perceived as poor or marginal credit risks.

The absence of pressure to generate profits also allowed retailers to offer very attractive interest rates in comparison with the rates on bank cards. They also did not have to charge an annual fee, which became a particularly strong selling point following the entrance of the third-party cards into the retail and gas markets. Since it did not cost the consumer anything to maintain a retail or gas card, both of which offered all the convenience of the bank cards but with lower rates, it made sense for the consumer not only to keep retail and gas cards but also to use them whenever shopping or buying gas.

The Retail Card Industry in the 1970s

At the beginning of the 1970s, retail stores dominated the credit card industry, in both cards outstanding and credit balances owed. My 1970 survey of several thousand households across the country (see Chapter 2) established that some 35 percent owned at least one retail card. In contrast, only 16 percent owned bank cards, and 9 percent owned T&E cards. Although 34 percent of families owned a gas card, gas cards were nowhere near the retail cards in terms of annual charges or outstanding balances.

Because credit customers constituted the traditional heart of their loyal customer base, retailers were resistant to the notion of accepting the credit of the "upstart" bank card companies. The 1970s, however, were marked by great changes in the use of credit cards by retailers, including the "defection" by J. C. Penney to the bank card, a move that would force the other major retailers to follow suit. Ironically, J. C. Penney was one of the earliest and most vocal opponents of bank cards being used in the retail industry. Kenneth Axelson, Penney's vice president and director of finance and administration, had said that his customers did not want "big brother" minding their business. He felt that the banks, rather than the customer, wanted all the customer's credit on one account. Before its 1979 agreement with Visa, Penney had resisted the incursion of bank cards largely because of its desire to make credit "responsive" to its merchandising plans and customer needs, as well as to keep a firmer hold on customers. Axelson stated that when people get overloaded with credit at one store, they go down the street to the next store and pay cash; a store relying on bank cards therefore risks losing customers who get behind in payments. If a customer falls behind in bank card payments, which represent the totality of credit, credit will be cut off and he or she can no longer buy at the store. A customer who always pays on time cannot make another purchase at the store once the credit limit is reached, even if the store is willing to extend the limit, because the bank and not the store controls that decision.

While the national retailers continued to oppose acceptance of third-party cards, the smaller regional or single-store retailers found such cards appealing. Since the operation of a credit department had substantial economies of scale, the smaller retailers quickly learned that it did not pay to handle their own accounts receivable. But since a large proportion of consumer goods were bought on credit, smaller retailers could not continue to operate without some kind of credit program. In addition, specialty stores that carried only certain types of merchandise were not so concerned about customer loyalty, since a customer would shop in such stores only occasionally. It was not realistic to assume that customers would carry store-specific charge cards to a sporting goods or furniture store that they visited only once or twice a year.

Given these circumstances, many smaller retailers were quite willing to honor third-party cards. By agreeing to accept bank cards, the retailer could not only be freed of the cost of operating a credit department but could also serve a wider market of credit customers who had them. Accepting bank cards was particularly attractive to stores located in tourist areas, since they could make credit sales to people from different cities, states, or even countries. During the early to mid-1970s, most smaller retailers began to accept bank cards, and often T&E cards as well.

As with the smaller retailers, the tremendous economies of scale in operating a credit operation placed it beyond the means of the larger, regional retailers as well. However, these companies were much more concerned about retaining customer loyalty and were unwilling to give the bank cards access to their markets. Furthermore, initial involvements with bank cards had proven unsatisfactory. In 1969, a Spokane, Washington retailer dropped its own credit card operation in favor of bank cards, only to see its charge sales plummet 46 percent. When the store's customers discovered that the bank cards began charging interest after thirty days rather than after sixty—the interest-free period they had previously received from the store—they stopped charging goods.

To solve the dilemma of the costs of running individual credit operations, the National Retail Merchants Association (NRMA) ran a test plan to pool its members' credit operations to cut costs while retaining an individual identity for each store. The trade association planned to arrange for credit suppliers other than banks to purchase the receivables of member stores. Including handling, billing, and collection, it was estimated that fees would range from 2.5 to 7.5 percent of average balances, depending on volume. An important consideration was retaining the logo of each store.

In 1971, NRMA gave a contract to the General Electric Credit Corporation (GECC) to design and test custom credit card services for NRMA members. The leader in private-label cards, GECC's approximately 300 clients included Federated Department Stores, Levitz Furniture, Gemco, and Singer. Its program for NRMA was designed primarily to meet the needs of small to medium-sized stores doing between $500,000 and $10 million annual volume and offered a comprehensive credit management package, including accounting, collection, billing, financing, and credit cards issued with each store's identification. GECC allowed retailers to take any part of the package or all of it and to pay a fixed "per account" fee, retaining all customer service charges for themselves. The only variable built into the plan was the cost of money, which would depend on average balance and whether the stores or GECC assumed the credit risk. When GECC undertook the NRMA project, it was already processing billings for over two million cardholder accounts through hundreds of small custom retail plans.

In 1972, Casual Corner, a women's clothing specialty chain that operated sixty-five stores in twenty-eight states, decided to turn over its 100,000 credit cards for handling by Custom Credit Card Service, a division of Shoppers Charge Service. Custom Credit Card Service was essentially a service bureau and credit management service. It allowed a retailer to offer a credit card under its own name, handle its own receivables and collections, and make its own credit decisions. A system was set up to handle regular, revolving, ninety-day, or fixed-payment plans complying with multistate credit regulations. Since each Casual Corner store was liable for its own bad debts, it could tailor its credit policies to meet local conditions. (This has proven to be a very successful plan of operation and is still used by a number of third-party companies like Custom Credit Card Service.)

Another credit card service offering private-label services was Chargette Independent Community Credit Cards, which was founded in 1957 to serve the Akron-Canton-Youngstown-Warren markets in Ohio. By 1971, the company had grown to 130,000 cardholders and had 28,000 active accounts. Approximately 1,100 merchants in the area honored its cards and provided customers with traditional thirty-day charge privileges plus a flexible charge plan offering payoff of the balance in five monthly installments.

Although private-label cards maintained retailers' identity with their customers, the private-label credit card services had the disadvantage of costing approximately one percent more than bank cards because of the smaller scale of their operations. That factor understandably slowed the spread of private-label credit card plans.

The major bank operating private-label programs in the early 1970s was Chase Manhattan, which handled credit cards for Two Guys, Times Square, Masters, and a number of other chains located primarily in the Northeast. In late 1975, Wells Fargo of San Francisco, the nation's eleventh-largest bank, signed an agreement with First Data Resources for a private-label program. The program, known as Well Service, handled private-label cards for a number of retailers. Retailers would return sales tickets to the bank, where amounts would be entered and balanced on video terminals on-line to the First Data Resources computer in Omaha, Nebraska. Credit authorization services, already provided to merchants participating in Wells Fargo's private-label plan, were also made available to all private-label clients.

In January 1977, GECC purchased from Woolworth $175 million in accounts receivable, which represented 1.1 million active accounts from Woolco and Woolworth operations in approximately 300 stores that offered credit services. Woolworth decided to continue to honor both Visa and Master Charge cards, while retaining its private-label cards.

The Cost to Retailers of Handling Credit

Both the growing acceptance of bank cards by retail merchants and the development of private-label cards were based on the presumed economies of scale in credit operations. Two important studies—"Economic Characteristics of Department Store Credit," which was carried out for the NRMA by the accounting firm of Touche, Ross, Bailey, and Smart in 1967, and "Retail Store Credit Card Use in New York" by Robert Shay and William C. Dunkelberg for Purdue's Credit Research Center—have shown that the cost to a retailer of extending credit is generally greater than the revenues received in interest on credit accounts. For small retailers, that cost is even greater.

According to the Touche, Ross study, the cost in 1967 of handling charge accounts for smaller retailers was $7.42 per account, as compared with $5.57 per account for larger retailers. The study also found:

Although small stores reported notably lower costs per account for establishing new accounts, large stores had lower costs per account for servicing and collection. As one might expect, costs per account of management services were lower for large stores. A large portion of the difference in costs per account appears to be explainable in terms of credit policy. Whereas small stores did not spend as much per account to screen applicants, they paid the price in collection costs. Costs of collection agencies and bad debts in thirty-day charge accounts amounted to 0.91 percent of these credit sales for small stores, compared to only 0.32 percent for large retailers.

The study pointed out that in terms of revenues, small stores were at a disadvantage compared with the larger retailers:

Service charge revenues averaged only 3.80 percent of credit sales, compared with 7.23 percent for large stores. . . . Among the revolving charge accounts of small stores, 44.5 percent of the account months had either no activity or nonrevolving balances compared with only 31.1 percent for the larger retailers. . . . In many cases, the small stores still had to process all accounts to determine whether balances were outstanding. Consequently, on over two-fifths of the account months for their revolving charge accounts, small retailers incurred costs but received no income.

Shay and Dunkelberg found that while most retailers do not break even on their credit operations, losses are larger for smaller retailers. They concluded:

Retail stores in New York do not collect sufficient finance charge revenues on their revolving credit accounts to cover the costs of extending and servicing such accounts. For the seventeen stores surveyed, the deficiency totalled $29 million or 3.71 percent of credit sales. Each of the seventeen stores incurred deficits on their revolving accounts. As a percent of sales, the largest deficits were incurred by small, independent stores upstate and the smallest deficits were incurred by national chain stores operating in the metropolitan region.

Therefore, if the deficiency for all retailers was 3.71 percent of credit sales, the deficiency for smaller retailers would be substantially higher. In the late 1960s and early 1970s, many small retailers overcame that deficiency by giving up their own credit operations. But did smaller retailers gain by relieving themselves of the costs of operating their own credit departments if they then had to pay merchant discounts on bank cards and T&E credit?

In most cases, merchant discounts are set locally and are negotiated and renegotiated between merchants and banks. According to the American Institute of Banking textbook *Bank Cards,* by this author and Neil B. Murphy, "Establishing the discount rate to merchants is greatly influenced by competitive conditions within the bank market area. The range is generally from 1 to 6 percent. In addition, the bank may establish a sliding scale depending on merchant volume and/or average ticket size."

Larger merchants paid a lower average discount to the banks than the smaller merchants because of their bargaining power and because of sliding scales based on volume. While many smaller merchants were hesitant to accept bank cards because of the relatively high discount rates they were forced to pay early in the 1970s, conditions changed substantially during the decade. As more and more banks launched credit card operations, the increased competition for merchant business caused the banks gradually to bid down discount rates to merchants.

The retailers' position was further enhanced in the mid-1970s by the onset of duality, which allowed banks to issue both Visa and Master Charge cards. Following Visa's 1976 decision to abandon its opposition to duality, immediate pressure was placed on banks to sign up merchants for both cards, since merchants understandably prefer to deposit the day's Visa and Master Charge slips in the same bank when that option became available. Thus, the effect of duality on merchants was to drive down discount rates even further.

By giving up their credit departments, smaller retailers ended up saving money, but at what cost? As observed earlier, one benefit to a retailer of extending its own credit was creating and sustaining customer loyalty. Yet, for small retailers with limited credit lines, loyalty is not quite as important as it is to the larger retailer that handles a great many lines. And before the J. C. Penney agreement with Visa, the fact that many large retailers did not accept bank cards was an advantage for the smaller stores, which gained a substantial edge over their larger competitors by accepting the universal bank cards, particularly from customers from outside the market area who did not carry the large regional retailer's credit card.

Following President Carter's 1980 announcement of credit restrictions on unsecured credit, the preliminary speculation in the press and elsewhere was that these controls might benefit larger retailers that issued their own credit, at the expense of small retailers dependent upon bank cards. According to a 1980 article in the *Wall Street Journal,* many retailers and analysts expect that department, chain, and specialty store credit cards will soon start replacing bank-issued cards which are fast becoming difficult to obtain and expensive to use. As a result, larger merchants that issue their own credit cards will gain business lost by small and medium-sized stores that rely on bank cards for most of their credit sales.

Because of credit restrictions, bank card companies began making their cards more expensive, by imposing annual fees, and issuing them more restrictively, thereby cutting off a sizable customer base for small retailers. The larger retailers, particularly the department stores, were able to overcome the new restrictions by selling an increasing number of durable goods on installment (i.e., secured) credit, thereby freeing up unsecured and unpenalized credit.

The smaller retailers, having abandoned their credit card operations, were totally dependent upon the credit card companies. The advantage they had gained over the larger retailers by accepting the cards had been largely negated by agreements such as the Visa-Penney accord. By the end of the decade, increased credit charges were driving many of their customers away, and some longtime customers were having their credit cut off by the bank card companies when they reached their charge limit, in spite of their good payment records. Increases in the merchant discount in the early 1980s added to the difficulties of some of the smaller retailers. Small retailers appear to have been whipsawed by the events of the 1970s.

The resistance of some of the larger department stores to third-party credit fell slightly in 1976, when Philadelphia department stores honored third-party credit cards as a "bicentennial gesture" primarily aimed at attracting the tourist trade. As a result of its success in catching some of the bicentennial tourist trade, Wanamaker's decided to accept American Express, Master Charge, and BankAmericard in all its Philadelphia stores on a permanent basis. Another Philadelphia store, Lits, decided to honor American Express only. Gimbels's Philadelphia store allowed customers who held an American Express, Diners Club, Visa, or Master Charge card to get a one-day courtesy charge, with a purchase limit of $100.

Throughout the 1970s, Sears continued to lead in both the retail credit card area and in the entire credit card industry. At the end of 1975, Sears announced that it had 21.6 million active cardholders with a total of thirty-three million cards outstanding and an annual charge volume in 1975 of $7.9 billion. J. C. Penney was next, with 10.5 million active accounts and an annual charge volume of $2.7 billion; Montgomery Ward had 6.5 million active accounts and an annual charge volume of $2.1 billion.

At that time, Sears had more active cardholders than either Master Charge or BankAmericard, making it the largest single credit card operation in the world. Its dominance of the retail credit card industry allowed it to pioneer certain actions that smaller competitors were unlikely to undertake by themselves. For example, in early 1974, Sears began to cut back promotion in certain states with restrictive usury laws, where maximum rates on credit ranged from 9 to 12 percent: Arkansas, Minnesota, South Dakota, Iowa, and Washington. Sears credit customers in these states were allowed to receive service, but now accounts were opened only on request. In addition, delinquent customers often found that their accounts were closed permanently. Sears maintained that cash customers in low-credit-rate states were subsidizing credit customers because the legal rates were too low to cover the costs of credit operation. Other large retailers followed Sears's action.

Given their sizable economies of scale and base of long-standing customers with outstanding balances, retail cards came closer to profitability than did the early bank cards. In 1975, Montgomery Ward reported that it just about broke even on its credit card operation, with a return of 0.4 percent on $2.6 billion of outstanding credit. Sears, on the other hand, reported a loss on its credit card operation in both 1975 and 1976; the loss, however, was much less than one percent of total credit volume outstanding. It should be noted that, given the usury battles that the big department stores were fighting in many states, it did not pay to show much profitability for their credit card operations. Slight adjustments in the attribution of fixed or joint costs could pretty much guarantee no embarrassing profits.

The Retail Card Industry in the 1980s

The historic agreement between J. C. Penney and Visa sest a new pattern in the field. Not only was it the first agreement between one of the big three nationwide retailers and a bank card company, but it was also the first direct contract between a retailer and a bank card company that bypassed the banks. A large chain operation had generally required a half-dozen banks to handle its business across the country, with each bank being given a percentage of the interchange volume. Penney, however, had a fully integrated electronic POS system with 23,000 terminals that could be modified to accept a bank card's magnetic stripe; it was therefore possible for all charges to be processed centrally and filed directly with a bank card company. By being the first of the big three retailers to sign with a bank card company, Penney obtained both a competitive jump in the marketplace and a special discount rate that would save it millions of dollars over the next several years.

As the 1970s ended, the feared takeover of retail credit cards by the bank cards had not materialized. Only the smaller retailers that could not afford to sustain their own credit operations depended upon the bank cards. A 1981 study found that of the nation's 100 largest department stores, only forty-eight took bank cards, while seventy-five accepted some third-party card, usually American Express.

Although the big three—Sears, J. C. Penney, and Montgomery Ward—did accept the bank cards, the general imposition of annual fees in 1979 meant that the "free" store cards were still prized by customers. In fact, Sears billed as many credit card customers each month as the total number of billings mailed by 12,000 member banks in either the Visa or MasterCard system. Of eighty-one million U.S. households, 57 percent had at least one Sears card in 1981, compared with Visa's figure of 53 percent, MasterCard's 47 percent percent, Penney's 39 percent, Ward's 27 percent, Federated's 17 percent, and American Express's 11 percent. With its huge customer base, it is not surprising that Sears followed the trend of other large financial institutions in diversifying its credit and (Allstate) insurance operations through the acquisition of the Coldwell Banker real estate firm and the Dean Witter brokerage.

In the 1980s, retail credit cards continued to perform well. Perhaps the most important development for the retail card industry as a whole has been the growth of third-party private-label cards. Private-label cards continue to function in much the same way as the original store cards. They allow the store to build customer loyalty and satisfaction without having to bear the burden of running the credit card operation. A survey done in the late 1980s for GECC's Retailer Financial Services by the research firm of Elrick and Lavidge showed that customers with a department store credit card spent approximately twice as much as customers without a store card and rated the store higher in all aspects of customer service. They also spent more than twice as much per year at the store than did customers who paid by other means.

GECC has been the leader in developing third party private-label cards. It gained a considerable number of cardholders in 1988 when it agreed to acquire the credit card portfolio of Montgomery Ward as part of the sale of the department store chain. The thirty-five million Ward cards added to the fifteen million private-label cards it already issued made GECC the nation's second-largest card issuer, after Sears.

Although GECC was the major player in the private-label business, it had an increasing amount of competition, particularly from the banks. In 1979, only 14 percent of banks issued private-label cards. In just six years, this proportion grew to 49 percent. However, it is not easy to get a customer to put another credit card into an already crowded wallet. To induce customers to do so, some stores began offering incentive packages, much as bank cards do. For example, Mervyn's, an apparel retailer in California, offered a 15 percent coupon to those who acquired its credit card and successfully increased store credit card sales.

As of 1988, Sears was still the leading issuer of credit cards in the United States, with more than eighty-four million in circulation (this figure includes Discover cards). It was followed by GECC with fifty million cards (thirty-five million of which were Montgomery Ward cards), J. C. Penney with forty-one and a half million, and Federated-Allied Stores with forty million. By comparison, Citibank, the leading bank issuer of credit cards, had only twenty-eight million in circulation, followed by Chase Manhattan Bank with 9.7 million cards.

Oil Company Credit Cards in the 1970s

Oil company "courtesy" cards were among the first credit cards issued on a widespread basis. From the inception of the automobile, the available supply of domestic gasoline has been more than adequate—except during wartime rationing—to meet demand at a relatively low price. Since one dealer's gasoline was essentially indistinguishable from another's and since price wars were destructive to all parties, other means of competition have always been preferred. One such means is the promotion of credit cards.

An advantage of oil company cards is that losses from fraud or charge-offs have been limited by the relatively low ticket size. When gasoline cost 25¢ per gallon, a full tank cost only a few dollars. Small tickets reduced the need for a quick and sophisticated authorization system. During the 1970s, the supply and price of gasoline changed dramatically, altering the structure of the industry and changing the position of the gas card.

Gas cards have always been money losers for the oil companies—their cost goes into the marketing budget. Even when the oil companies moved to a revolving charge system, the very low ticket and balance size made the interest charges little more than added incentive for customers to pay promptly. A variety of ideas have been tried in an attempt to lower losses on the cards, such as expanding the merchant base to include other travel-related expenses such as motels, and using the cards to sell tangentially related or nonrelated goods and services to the cardholder.

Losses on oil company credit cards in 1971 were the highest ever. Although many oil companies wanted to drop their credit card operations entirely, a substantial marketing advantage accrued to the cards because gasoline was relatively homogeneous and marketing people were hard-pressed to find a substitute for credit cards to create brand loyalty. In addition, customer credit card lists proved to be highly profitable for mail-order sales of merchandise and services, although that revenue did not come close to offsetting credit card losses. Quite simply, the economics of oil company credit cards—low ticket purchases and high processing costs—made the possibility of profitable credit card operations unlikely.

Rather than eliminate the cards altogether, many oil companies began to limit their operations in an effort to control costs and restrict the outstanding balances on their cards.

In 1971, Atlantic Richfield set a precedent by turning over its entire credit card operation to an outside firm, National Data Corporation of Atlanta, Georgia. National Data promised to handle the billing on a unified and nationwide basis through what it termed a "greatly advanced system." In 1972, Atlantic Richfield dropped the financing of receivables from motel chains.

That same year, in an effort to reduce losses on its credit card sales, Shell Oil Company notified its dealers that they would have to pay a one percent service fee on Shell credit card sales and half the cost of the bank card discount. The action was immediately challenged by President Nixon's Federal Price Commission as being an increase in price. This challenge, combined with the very unfavorable reaction from Shell franchise dealers, led the company to delay the action.

☐ **Political Upheaval: The Gas Crises of 1973 and 1979**
As a result of the Arab oil embargo in 1973, many drivers found that they could not purchase gasoline at their usual stations. Those who traditionally bought on credit were therefore prompted to apply for as many additional credit cards as they could. A survey of major oil companies indicated an influx of new applications that could not be attributed to other causes.

The unique environment in which oil company credit cards operated made it very difficult for them to achieve profitability. Gasoline stations tended to have a high turnover of employees who were poorly paid and had little incentive to spot misused credit cards. Furthermore, the nature of gasoline sales made the use of printed warning bulletins impossible. On-line authorization systems were not cost-justified, and the cost of collecting past-due balances exceeded the size of most of the balances. When these problems were combined with the boycott of 1973–74, oil companies began refusing to honor credit cards other than their own.

Major oil firms had begun to accept third-party credit cards issued by banks and T&E companies during the late 1960s in an effort to expand gasoline sales and to reduce their financing of credit receivables. However, once the glut of oil turned into a limited supply situation, the marketing motivation for accepting third-party credit cards was greatly reduced, as was the incentive for oil companies to honor other gas credit cards. In addition, some dealers who were charged part of the cost of accepting their own oil company's credit card stopped accepting it. Others demanded payment in cash to speed the long lines waiting at the pumps.

One unanticipated result of the oil shortage was that delinquencies on oil company credit cards went down. Cardholders presumably had an additional incentive to keep up with their payments so that they could use their card whenever they had the opportunity to buy some gas. The oil crisis also precipitated the cancellation of reciprocal agreements to honor the credit cards of other oil companies.

The oil crisis after the 1979 Iranian revolution was similar to the embargo crisis five years earlier. Between 1974 and 1979, many persons who had obtained a variety of gas cards in response to the earlier oil crisis had reverted to using their bank credit cards. The oil companies, which had discontinued acceptance of bank cards, were compelled to begin accepting them again to compete for business. With gas lines forming again in 1979, the cycle began to repeat itself. Consumers applied for many oil company cards, and the oil companies began to refuse bank cards. In late summer of 1979, both Mobil and Texaco dropped bank cards, and others soon followed.

For most of the oil companies, not accepting bank cards was welcome relief. In 1978, more than one-quarter of the 117 billion gallons of gasoline sold for passenger car use in the United States had been charged to credit cards. Over 13.5 billion gallons ($20.6 billion in credit sales) were charged on Visa or Master Charge. Oil companies or the dealers who honored bank cards paid $63 million to banks in merchant fees. In 1979, the oil companies estimated that the business they received from bank cards would cost them about $163 million, and that was with only four of the eight major refiners honoring them.

Because of the increasing use of bank cards for gasoline, it was anticipated that by 1985 oil companies would be spending $695 million annually in the form of merchant discounts to the bank card companies for gasoline purchases. The gas shortage in the wake of the 1979 oil crisis allowed the oil companies to once again refuse to accept the bank cards.

Merchant discounts were not the only factor leading to the banning of bank cards from gasoline stations. For example, Mobil dropped bank credit cards because of the authorization procedures of the bank card companies. Bank card sales over $25 had to be either checked against hot card lists or cleared by phone. Both procedures were time-consuming, particularly outdoors in bad weather when motorists were waiting in long lines for service. Gasoline price increases raised the average sale from $6.50 ten years before to $12.30 in 1979. That increase boosted the number of credit authorizations and the size of charge-backs to oil companies by enormous proportions. Nonetheless, the charge-back rate on gas cards averaged only about 0.7 percent of charge volume, a far lower figure than that experienced by the bank and T&E card companies.

From 1978 to 1980, the structure of the gasoline industry changed dramatically, with accompanying effects on credit cards. Not only did the price of gasoline double, but a 10 percent decrease in the number of pump locations caused consumers to increase the average purchase from 10 to 11.7 gallons. Yet, because of restrictions on issuance, the number of cards outstanding dropped from 126 million to 110 million. With fewer customers running up higher hills, the average monthly statement went from $21.64 to $49.72.

But these changes did not go far toward making the gas cards profitable on a stand-alone basis. Other factors, such as increased postal rates, boosted costs. Largely for that reason, Chevron, the nation's thirteenth-largest grantor of credit with 8.5 million cards outstanding, discontinued the use of billing stuffers with monthly statements. Merchandising had once been a lucrative sideline to the credit card business, but the popularity of such programs among virtually all credit card issuers had decreased returns. In addition, higher gasoline prices apparently caused cardholders to cut back on the nonessential or impulse offers that worked best in the billing stuffers.

On 1 November 1981, Texaco took a step away from the card business by imposing a 3 percent fee on dealers for processing Texaco gas card transactions. Given the extremely low markup on gasoline, the 3 percent fee cost many dealers their entire profit. Since usury laws in most states prohibited a surcharge for the use of a credit card, the dealers were faced with three alternatives. They could refuse to accept the cards, they could accept the cards and reduce their profit, or they could give a discount for cash. Late in 1976, Exxon had experimented with a cash discount for customers who did not use credit cards. The experiment was run by twenty dealers in Abilene, Texas, and thirty-two dealers in Charleston, South Carolina, but was not widely used at the time.

Some Texaco stations in 1981 accepted the cards in their full-service sections only, not in self-service sections. Another move by Texaco was to accept bank cards. It was the first major oil company to begin accepting bank cards since the beginning of the 1979 embargo. The move was prompted in part by the fact that in some states, such as Texas, 40 to 50 percent of retail gasoline sales were made on credit cards.

Rather than seek ways to limit credit card use, several oil companies decided to eliminate cards entirely. On 15 April 1982, Atlantic Richfield became the first major oil company to drop its credit card. With 6.1 million cardholders, it had been the eighth-largest issuer of gas cards but ranked only eleventh in volume among the twenty-two largest oil company credit card issuers. Dealers were permitted to accept third-party cards if they were willing to pay the merchant discount.

The pattern established in the early 1980s continues today. A few oil companies, such as Atlantic Richfield, do not issue cards. Others, such as Texaco, charge different prices for cash and charge purchases, while a third group, which includes Sunoco, for instance, do not differentiate. By 1987, there were over 100 million gas cards in circulation in the United States. Amoco, with 22 million cards, was the largest gas card issuer. It was followed by Shell with 15 million and Mobil with 14.2 million. Texaco was fourth with 13 million, followed by Chevron (12.6 million) and Exxon (12 million.)

Despite the growing number of cards in circulation, the dollar volume on gas cards dropped from $28.9 billion in 1980 to $24.1 billion in 1987, partly because of falling energy prices, but also because of an increased number of bank card transactions. The dollar volume on gas cards also continues to lag far behind that of bank cards. Although the gas cards generate a high number of transactions, the average ticket size is much smaller than that for bank cards. A number of oil companies have been prompted to develop more efficient POS systems that can support both credit and debit cards. In 1987, Mobil introduced its Mobil Plus card, which not only allows its holder to charge gasoline but also to obtain cash advances of up to $20. Although Mobil did not charge a lower price for cash sales, it did institute a $12 annual fee to cover the cost of its new system. Exxon has begun a similar system, but without the annual fee.

8

Travel and Entertainment Cards

IN 1970, THERE WERE FIVE MAJOR TRAVEL and entertainment cards competing for dominance in the narrowing worldwide T&E business: American Express, Diners Club, Carte Blanche, EuroCard, and the Universal Air Travel Plan (UATP) run by the airlines. At the time, there was a clear difference between the bank cards and the T&Es: the latter charged an annual fee and offered credit limits that were far greater than those offered by the banks. The T&Es were not seen as being competitive with the bank cards because they were used largely by businesspeople and the bank cards were still primarily "consumer" cards.

It was not unusual at that time for a consumer to possess both major bank cards (BankAmericard and Master Charge). Because they were "free," that is, the banks did not charge an annual fee for them, it did not cost the consumer any more to possess two cards than it did to own one. The similar services and benefits of T&E cards, however, coupled with their annual fees, gave consumers little incentive to sign up for more than one T&E card. That fact was a major contribution to the steady consolidation of the industry in the 1970s, when it appeared unlikely that more than one company could survive over the long run. In the early 1960s, one out of every three T&E cardholders carried more than one T&E card; by 1972, that ratio had dropped to one out of eleven cardholders.

As the decade began, the company that seemed the most likely to exploit the trend toward consolidation was American Express. With over 2.5 million cardholders in the United States, American Express was already more than twice the size of Diners Club, and four times the size of Carte Blanche. Moreover, both Diners Club and Carte Blanche were facing difficult times.

After its ill-fated and expensive attempt to restore the *Queen Mary*, Diners Club experienced one of its worst years ever in 1970. For the nine-month period ending 31 December 1970, the company reported record losses of $31.1 million, while memberships were decreasing at a rate of 5,000 per week. In an attempt to staunch these staggering losses, R. Newell Lusby was recruited from the parent Continental Insurance Company ranks to head up the ailing subsidiary, replacing George Faunce III as president.

There was substantial speculation that Diners Club would fold, but Continental Insurance was having a difficult time finding someone to take over the $300–400 million in receivables. It is not easy to sell a credit card company because the bulk of its assets are the receivables, which are particularly difficult to collect if the card is terminated. In May 1971, Chase Manhattan's name surfaced as a possible candidate to acquire Diners Club. However, the estimated asking price of $100 million was too high to interest Chase.

The deteriorating situation of Diners Club in the United States had repercussions in the still profitable Diners Club franchise operations abroad. At that time, Diners Club was still the dominant credit card company in Europe. Its concept of local management, financing, and control had enabled it to flourish in the European environment. Its franchises issued cards in twenty-four European countries, and its cards were honored throughout the Continent. European charge volume in 1971 was $245 million. In contrast, American Express was still experiencing difficulty in building a significant cardholder base anywhere but in Great Britain, partly because of the centralized control that it exerted from its London office. In the early 1970s, American Express had fewer than 70,000 cardholders in Europe, and half of them were in England.

Despite Diners Club's strength overseas, its domestic problems eventually undercut its European operations. Franchisees found that the dwindling membership in the United States led to decreased charge volume from U.S. cardholders traveling abroad. On the other side of the ocean, the decreasing number of U.S. establishments that honored Diners Club cards created dissatisfaction for foreign cardholders traveling in America. Franchise owners in thirty-seven countries had their fortunes directly tied to the success or failure of the U.S. operation, and they were angered by what they perceived to be mismanagement of that operation. Led by Horatio Klabin, franchisee for Brazil, Portugal, and Germany, foreign franchise holders charged mismanagement and lack of support by the parent company. Klabin threatened to withhold commission payments unless the situation was corrected.

The company finally hit bottom late in the fall of 1971. In the first three-quarters of that year, Diners Club lost more than $15 million. It was also reported that Diners Club Argentina, of which Diners Club U.S.A. owned 76 percent, was near bankruptcy. To help the company back onto its feet, Lusby requested $25 million from Continental Insurance. Continental turned him down flat, leaving him to solve the company's problems on his own.

Miraculously, even without the support of Diners Club's parent company, Lusby was able to significantly improve the company's performance by early 1972. The turnaround resulted from a number of actions, including the elimination of unprofitable subsidiaries and departments, tightening fraud control, reducing executive staff, and greatly increasing efficiency in handling customer billing and collection through the new Denver Credit Card Center. The last move solved the enormous communication tie-ups and union problems that had plagued the company when it was located at New York's Columbus Circle. Also contributing to a brighter picture was the turnaround of Diners Club's collection subsidiary, National Account Systems, which came out of deep red figures to near profitable operations for the first time since it was acquired.

Another significant reason for the turnaround of Diners Club was the cut in its credit losses from 4.75 percent to 0.65 percent from 1971 to 1973. Fraud losses were reduced by innovative mailing procedures, such as the use of dual-dated cards with post-mailers. Cards were mailed approximately two and a half weeks before they became valid, and post-mailers were also sent out so that cardholders could notify Diners Club if their cards had not yet been received.

By mid-1972, management and financial problems for almost all of the Diners Club's franchises had been resolved, and collectively, they were at a record level of membership volume and profit. During the first six months of 1972, Diners Club losses were down to $4.4 million, compared with $10.3 million during the same period the year before, and although the company ended 1972 with a net loss of $7.3 million, that figure was less than a third of 1971's net loss. In the six months ending 31 July 1973, Diners Club was back in the black for the first time since 1969, showing a consolidated net profit of $449,000, compared with a loss of $4.4 million in the same period the year before. In addition, customer complaints, which had once run over 4,000 per month, were down to an estimated 300 per month.

While Diners Club had tried to solve its problems by improving its domestic operations, Carte Blanche responded to its dwindling card-holder base in the United States by concentrating its efforts abroad. The company's president, Jim Hawthorne, initiated an aggressive expansion program abroad. Hawthorne believed that foreign bankers did not understand revolving credit. They did not like bank card economics, and many did not want the name of an American bank associated with their company. For the most part, foreign bankers saw the advantage of a "fee" card, but not a "free" card.

Hawthorne's new program produced several successes, particularly in South America. However, before he could implement further changes he was replaced in late 1971 by Lorne Fonteyne as head of day-to-day operations. Fonteyne's orientation was marketing, and he was brought in to promote the card domestically and abroad. The parent company, Avco, had apparently reevaluated the potential of the credit card business in view of Carte Blanche's steady gain on Diners Club and its profitability after four years of losses. In addition, Carte Blanche's recent success in signing up franchises abroad presented the opportunity to become the number-two T&E company internationally.

By the summer of 1972, Carte Blanche was still in third place in Europe among the T&E issuers, but rapidly closing the gap. It was now honored in about 30,000 establishments in Europe, compared with only about 5,000 three years earlier. Of the three T&E cards, Carte Blanche was generally regarded as more prestigious than American Express and Diners Club. But prestige was of limited help with merchants who no longer wanted to bother with the bookkeeping associated with multiple-card systems.

In October 1972, Carte Blanche began issuing its Gold Club card to members who maintained good credit standing and met certain payment ratios. (The notion of a special card had been rejected by Diners Club in 1968 because its executives thought that visible recognition of preferential treatment for some members would create problems.) The Gold Club card was issued for a period of two years rather than one. The response to the Carte Blanche Gold Club card was favorable. The company received numerous compliments and letters of appreciation from members, as well as requests from people who had noticed their friends carrying the card and wanted one for themselves.

Early in 1973, Fonteyne left the presidency of Carte Blanche to take over Avco Savings and Loan, headquartered in California. He left the firm in good shape: Carte Blanche would continue its growth in cardholders and earnings, which reached a record after-tax level of $1.1 million in 1972. The temporary success of Carte Blanche probably resulted from a renewed consumer interest in a prestige card, as well as from its effective promotional program.

The turnaround in Carte Blanche unfortunately coincided with a downturn in the fortunes of Avco, its parent company, which lost $18.3 million in fiscal 1973. Avco nearly sold the credit card operation to Thomas Cook in April 1974. However, when confronted with the economics of selling a credit card operation, that is, with the heavy discounting of accounts receivable, Avco decided to hold onto Carte Blanche for the time being. The credit card company was left with the problem of retaining member establishments and building charge volume without adequate resources from the strapped parent company.

P. Kenneth Dunsire was brought in as the new president of Carte Blanche, succeeding Keith Rowan, who had briefly succeeded Lorne Fonteyne. Dunsire had previously been vice president for marketing and used his skills to increase the number of cardholders and bring the operation briefly back into the black in 1975.

Despite the various attempts, and limited success, of both Carte Blanche and Diners Club to regain market share in the T&E card industry, none of their efforts seemed capable of slowing American Express's seemingly inexorable annexation of the entire marketplace. By the end of 1976, American Express had 6.3 million cardholders in the United States, compared with 837,000 for Diners Club and 640,000 for Carte Blanche, a decrease of more than 100,000 from 1973. On a worldwide basis, American Express also dominated the T&E industry with nearly eight of the eleven million cards in circulation. Diners Club accounted for 2.3 million, and Carte Blanche had only 660,000. American Express's 1977 sales volume of $8.3 billion, while still less than Master Charge's $14.8 billion and Visa's $12.5 billion, was ten and twenty times higher than Diners Club and Carte Blanche, respectively.

A significant reason for American Express's domination of the industry, in both billings and cardholders, was its ability to develop and successfully implement new programs. It also showed itself to be adept at expanding and improving upon new programs developed by its competitors. In 1975, American Express launched its own gold card in response to Carte Blanche's similarly named plan. It added a magnetic stripe to the back of its cards, allowing cardholders to take advantage of the rapidly expanding network of ATMs and cash dispensers. The company also began installing in airports around the country traveler's check dispensers that could be activated by its new gold card as well as the green card.

Another very successful program developed by American Express was its corporate card program. As noted earlier, the T&E card was used primarily by businesspeople. Recognizing that fact, American Express began its corporate card program in 1966. The primary difference between the corporate card and American Express's other cards was that a corporation was responsible for the cards of all of its employees. The plan saved American Express the expense of running separate credit checks on each employee cardholder—normally between $3 and $8 per credit check.

By 1975, American Express had some 200,000 corporate customers who accounted for 28 percent of total cardholders. Most corporate accounts were small, however, averaging fewer than two cards per account. In the fall of 1975, American Express decided to pursue corporate accounts more aggressively; they produced more profit because of lower collection problems and they had brought in three times the volume of the noncorporate accounts. A major direct-marketing program that involved calling on companies expanded the total number of corporate cards by about one-third.

In 1976 and 1977, American Express began pushing hard to get its cards into major department and specialty stores; the company wanted these stores to honor its cards exclusively, or in addition to the private-label store cards. During a fourteen-month period beginning in January 1976, twenty-one stores signed with American Express, compared with a total of only seven in the previous three years. To aid its campaign, American Express developed local television spot commercials that were integrated with the store's advertising. This type of joint promotion would become a marketing trademark of American Express in future years.

In 1977, American Express added a new emergency check-cashing service through all American Airlines airport ticket counters in the United States. American Airlines would cash personal checks for American Express cardholders holding a ticket on any regularly scheduled flight leaving within forty-eight hours or completed in the previous forty-eight hours.

That same year, American Express added Centurion Service for its cardholders. For $300 a year, the top executives of large corporations would be offered special benefits such as special room bookings, theater tickets, golf and tennis reservations, stenographic services, and so on. Centurion Service did what American Express was already doing through its travel and ticket offices, but the prestige package was structured to appeal to business executives who wanted the best. The new service also further differentiated the T&E card from the "lowly" bank card.

A significant selling point for the American Express Gold card over its green card was the line of credit offered to Gold cardholders. To extend credit to its Gold cardholders, American Express entered into agreements with numerous banks around the world whereby American Express would still receive the merchant discount on the cards but the interest on the revolving balances would be taken by the banks. By June of 1979, more than 1,400 banks were enrolled in the American Express Gold card plan, and most of them issued Visa and MasterCard as well. A number of S&Ls and credit unions also offered gold cards to their members.

The Amex Gold card allowed the participating banks to offer their customers what the bank cards lacked, a combination of prestige and higher credit limits. The credit line for Gold cardholders started at $2,000 and averaged twice that, although some institutions went as high as $15,000. Gold cardholders could get up to $500 per week in traveler's checks from machines at more than 100 airports and other significant travel locations in the United States and Canada, and up to $1,000 a week at American Express travel offices worldwide and at the offices of participating banks.

From the banks' standpoint, the Amex Gold cards generated revenue in addition to providing customer benefits. American Express paid them $12.50 for each new cardholder, plus $5 per year for renewals. American Express also paid 25–50¢ per transaction on cash dispensers away from the cardholder's home city. Furthermore, banks were given the opportunity to draw on a promotion allowance of up to $5 per year per account, and for special promotions to Visa and MasterCard cardholders, American Express picked up the entire cost.

By the mid-1970s, as American Express continued to extend its domination over the T&E industry, both Avco and Continental Insurance decided to spin off their T&E operations. Although both Diners Club and Carte Blanche were profitable, the parent companies realized that they did not have the resources to compete effectively against American Express for very long.

Avco was the first to succeed in divesting itself of its T&E operation. In 1975, it entered into negotiations with Citibank to sell Carte Blanche. Citibank was a natural choice to acquire the T&E company. It had owned Carte Blanche for a brief time in the 1960s but was forced to divest itself of the card operation by the Justice Department, which found the combination anticompetitive. Therefore, Citibank sold Carte Blanche to Avco in 1968. By 1975, however, conditions in the T&E industry had been changed dramatically by the dominance of American Express. Introducing a second major player into the T&E area was definitely considered pro-competitive.

Citibank had a number of reasons for making the acquisition. Taking on Carte Blanche would give it a chance to shift gradually away from the free credit card business without attracting the type of negative publicity generated by its abortive 50-cent charge for bank cardholders who had no interest charges on their revolving accounts. In addition, then–Vice President John Reed wanted to compete head-on with American Express in dispensing Citibank traveler's checks in airports. The acquisition also gave Citibank an opportunity to use its foreign banking offices as promotion centers for the foreign business of Carte Blanche, which would enable it to develop an international prestige card market. In the long run, Citibank would be able to circumvent prohibitions on interstate banking by building up an affluent retail customer base through the Carte Blanche card.

Fearing its competitive potential, American Express filed suit to block the Citibank acquisition, on the grounds that it was anti-competitive. American Express reasoned that, with its Visa and MasterCard franchises, Citibank would issue three of the five major credit cards in the United States. Furthermore, the merging of Carte Blanche with Citibank's other card operations would presumably weaken the competitive position of Carte Blanche.

In 1978, Citibank was finally given unconditional permission to make the acquisition. The acquisition price was paid entirely in cash. Citibank, however, refused to divulge the final price, noting only that the amount was "insignificant" by Citibank standards. Following its acquisition, Citibank started an aggressive campaign to boost market share in the United States while expanding overseas outlets. Under its new president, Truman Sussman, it lowered the price of the Carte Blanche/Citicard to a dollar per month, undercutting American Express by more than 50 percent. At the same time, advertising stressed the prestige of owning the new card. The campaign was successful, and by the spring of 1980, Carte Blanche membership had been boosted by one-third to nearly one million.

While Citibank's acquisition of Carte Blanche was not seen as detrimental to either American Express or the industry in general, its immediate effect was to put pressure on Continental to sell Diners Club as quickly as possible, since it was now competing with two financial services giants in the T&E business. By the late 1970s, Diners Club's remarkable turnaround had come to an end. As in earlier years, the overseas franchises were doing well with their own cardholders but were suffering from a dwindling tourist business from the United States, where Diners Club's cardholder base continued to decline. The loss of cardholders quickly snowballed: merchants dropped out of the plan because fewer customers carried the card, leading even more cardholders to turn in their cards because fewer and fewer merchants now honored them. Cardholders saw no point in paying the annual $25 fee for a card they could not use.

In an attempt to shore up its sagging operations, Diners Club linked up with Chase Manhattan Bank in 1978 to offer a line of credit ranging from $2,000 to $25,000 for Diners Club members, which could be paid back at the rate of 12 percent annually on the outstanding balance using special checks issued by Chase Manhattan. That move was designed to make Diners Club competitive with the American Express Gold card. However, the program failed to attract new cardholders and lost money for both Chase and Diners Club.

Early in 1979, David Gray, who had taken over from Newell Lusby, was replaced by Sy Flug as president of Diners Club. By 1979, Diners Club was continuing to survive only through its forty-four franchises and twelve agencies abroad, which were growing at 15 percent per year in cardholders and at more than 30 percent per year in charge volume from the 1.7 million cardholders in 115 countries. The only solution seemed to be to sell the operation, and the most likely candidate appeared to be Chase, which had tried to buy Diners Club in 1965. However, its bad experience cosponsoring the line-of-credit promotion with Diners Club convinced Chase to back away from a permanent relationship. Other takeover possibilities were reported to be Continental Bank in Chicago and Bank of America.

On 12 December 1980, in a surprise move, Diners Club was purchased by Citibank, which had acquired Carte Blanche just two years before. For less than $20 million, Citibank added 900,000 fee-paying customers to its T&E system. Given the weak position of Diners Club and the strong positions of American Express, Visa, and MasterCard, the acquisition did not generate much opposition from the Justice Department.

Citibank continued to operate both cards as separate entities throughout the 1980s, although much of the actual operations were merged. Of the two, Diners Club has proved a much more successful operation. By the end of 1987, it had just under 1.2 million cards outstanding, with an annualized charge volume of $4.9 billion, while Carte Blanche had only 155,000 cards in circulation (only 35,000 in the United States), with an annualized charge volume of $112 million— equal to just 0.1 percent of the market. Neither card has seriously challenged American Express for the T&E market. For example, in the upscale market (which includes the American Express, Visa, and MasterCard Gold cards), Diners Club and Carte Blanche combined for only 4.2 percent of the total charge volume in 1987.

Profitability

Despite all of the problems experienced by Carte Blanche and Diners Club, both were profitable operations for much of the 1970s. The same could not be said for even the most successful bank card programs, which, as we have seen, operated for most of that decade in the red. A primary reason that the T&E cards were better able to achieve profitability lay in the methods they used to derive their operating income. Annual fees on T&E cards in 1977 averaged $17.69 per card, allowing for reduced fees on multiple accounts. That fee was collected up front at the beginning of the year. Banks, meanwhile, collected an average of $88.20 in interest per year from active cardholders with unpaid balances, but since more than half their customers paid in full every month, the average interest fee on all active accounts was less than half that figure.

T&E cards also had much lower operating expenses than bank cards. Expenses for the T&Es were lower as the result of greater cardholder selectivity, which cost the T&E cards only 0.98 percent of volume in delinquencies, overspending, and fraud loss, as compared with 1.29 percent of volume for bank cards. In addition, the banks had eight times as many active accounts and more than eight times as many transactions, which together produced less than three times the charge volume of the T&Es. The average T&E card charge of $59.66 was more than twice as high as the average bank card charge of $27. In addition, the average T&E monthly statement of $136.70 in current charges was almost twice as high as the $74.25 in the average bank card statement, and it could be processed and billed for under one-half the cost of the bank card statement.

Not only were T&E card expenses much lower, but income from merchant discounts was substantially greater than it was with the bank cards. The T&Es charged a minimum discount of 3.5 percent, except for special deals to hotels and airlines, and an average of 5.5 percent across the board. The bank cards, which were far more competitive, charged rates as low as 1.75 percent in the highly contested markets of New York, Chicago, and Los Angeles.

Despite their advantages over bank cards, the T&E cards have faced a strong challenge from the banks in recent years. Having secured control of the lower and middle ends of the credit card market, both Visa and MasterCard have launched their own gold cards to compete with the T&E companies for the prestige card market. By 1988, the bank gold cards had garnered 37 percent of the prestige market (see also Chapter 6).

The Airline Travel Cards

A generally unnoticed but important factor in the T&E market has been the airline travel cards: those issued by individual airlines, and those issued by the Universal Air Travel Plan. UATP was launched in the late 1930s; by the end of 1970, UATP and its airline travel card had 1.7 million cardholders and 120,000 subscriber accounts.

Initially, the plan had levied a $425 charge that was kept on account to be drawn against whenever a cardholder booked a flight. Over the years, the deposit of $425 did not change, but it did pay interest. The rules governing the account were administered by the Civil Aeronautics Board (CAB), although UATP was administered by the Air Traffic Conference of America—a division of the International Air Transport Association (IATA)—which, by 1970 included 130 airlines. Nearly 90 percent of cardholders came from just four airlines: American, United, TWA, and Eastern.

Promotion of the joint airline travel card had ceased around 1960 when airlines began promoting their own cards. Nonetheless, the UATP continued to generate the bulk of charge purchases for the airlines, with a 1970 total of $1.3 billion. UATP passed up the temptation to become a true T&E card by signing up other travel-related businesses, such as hotels and rental cars, since its airline members wanted to retain that business for themselves.

While UATP provided the airlines with a vehicle for facilitating credit sales, it did little to help individuals airlines keep or extend market share. For that reason, a number of airlines began to issue their own cards. In April 1966, United Airlines began to promote its private card to college students along its main routes. The appeal of students was that they were likely to remain loyal to the airline after graduation. In 1970, TWA turned its private airline card into a T&E card. By the end of that year, there were more than 500,000 TWA Get-Away cardholders.

In early 1971, the airlines issued specifications for standardization of their credit cards, which included a magnetic stripe for encoding. Many airlines were anxious to stop accepting the outside T&E cards because of the merchant discount of about 3 percent. They preferred the bank cards because the standard airline discount for BankAmericard and Master Charge at the end of 1970 was 2 percent, and a few Master Charge banks still gave United Airlines one percent. Another factor linking the airlines to bank cards was the fact that some banks that issued the cards also supplied the loans needed by the airlines for their equipment. On 1 July 1971, the airlines began issuing air travel cards with both the IATA and the ABA magnetic stripes.

In late 1973, UATP began to expand into the T&E market with its new silver airline travel card. The expansion was seen as a matter of survival: volume on the airline travel cards had been virtually flat since 1970, while the bank and T&E cards had experienced substantial growth. As anticipated, the UATP Silver card was opposed by Bank-Americard, Master Charge, and other credit card issuers, as well as by the American Society of Travel Agents because it did not get a commission on non-tour UATP tickets. A major supporter of the UATP's Silver card was TWA, which had achieved success on its private Get-Away card and believed that an industrywide card would be helpful in lowering the discounts paid on the bank and T&E cards. Market studies found that 80 percent of TWA's cards were used for TWA travel, which made a strong case for the value of a private-label airline card coexisting with an industrywide airline travel silver card on which TWA tickets could be charged without imposition of the substantial discounts charged on T&E and bank cards.

On 8 August 1975, the CAB gave the UATP Silver card preliminary permission to proceed. The card could be used in hotels and for car rentals in addition to air travel on 180 airline members of UATP. As a further benefit, there was no annual fee, and in fact, cardholders were given a one percent discount on their airfares. A lawsuit to block the card on antitrust grounds was filed by American Express, which was joined in that effort by Diners Club, Carte Blanche, Visa, and MasterCard, all of whom argued that it would restrict competition. On 12 June 1980, the CAB issued a ruling that the UATP Silver card promoted competition and gave it final approval.

American Express continued to dominate the T&E industry throughout the 1980s, growing with the tremendous boom in the early years of the decade and weathering the stock market setback to its brokerage business in late 1987. Ironically, it was the company's travel-related business that helped it through the down period of the late 1980s and was responsible for virtually all of its net income. Diners Club and Carte Blanche both suffered through that period, in large part because the travel focus of the cards was lost when they were acquired by large conglomerates.

The reasons for American Express's long-term success in the T&E field are many. An obvious one is the company's significant financial muscle, which provided the ready source of capital necessary to launch a credit card operation. Perhaps most importantly, American Express built its card expertise in an industry in which it was already a leader, the travel finance industry. When it began its card operation in the 1950s, it had offices in most major cities and a clientele of upscale cusomters who were dependent upon its services. Finally, the company was motivated by the very real fear that it could lose its dominance to a superior payment mechanism unless it made a strong move into the credit card industry. As the 1980s drew to a close, however, American Express suddenly found itself in competition with two opponents that could match its financial resources—Visa and MasterCard.

9

The Impact of Technology

IN EARLY 1965, JOHN SHEPERD-BARRON, managing director of De La Rue Instruments, a small division of De La Rue Company of London, England, was mulling over the possible uses of a new invention his division had just perfected. Working for Shell Oil, they had just completed work on a prototype gas dispenser that used noncounterfeitable tokens instead of cash. Sheperd-Barron was convinced that there were many other applications for De La Rue's new machine. Knowing that his company also made cash-handling machines for the commercial banks, he made the "logical jump . . . to 'through-the-wall' cash dispensing," as he later recalled.

The next day he had lunch with the chief executive of Barclay's Bank, the world's fourth-largest bank at that time. Sheperd-Barron put forth a plan for the bank to produce a cash dispenser that would be activated by a check and would issue a standard amount of £10 per check. He later recalled:

> Ninety-five seconds into my spiel, he stopped me and said if we could have that he would back me up all the way, but wanted our exclusive agreement in order to get a head start on the competition. What I did not know at the time was the London Clearing Banks had quietly decided to close on Saturdays, but were anxious as to the effect on their customers—this idea if implemented nationally could defuse customer ire.

De La Rue quickly assembled six prototypes of the new machines. Based upon its functionality, De La Rue received a letter of intent from Barclay's for seventy-five machines. The first through-the-wall cash dispenser in the world went live in June 1967 in Enfield near London. Shortly thereafter, another machine was installed at the Union Bank of Switzerland in the Bahnofstrasse, Zurich. The De La Rue machines read an engraved piece of script that looked more like a traveler's check than a card. Chubb of Great Britain, with National Westminster Bank, soon introduced its own machine, which was activated by a magnetic card.

The First ATMS in the United States

It did not take long for the new technology to make its way across the Atlantic to the United States. That same year, in 1965, a new type of dispensing machine, known as the automated teller machine (ATM), was unveiled at the American Bankers Association (ABA) automation conference. Dubbed the Satellite, it had been developed by Diebold. Unlike the cash dispenser, which simply gave out cash, the ATM handled payments, transfers, and deposits as well as cash dispensing, using a standard credit card. It even had an optional teller video assist.

The first U.S. company to enter this new field was Docutel of Dallas, Texas. Launched in May 1967 by Recognition Equipment, Inc., Docutel was formed to develop, manufacture, and market airline baggage-handling equipment. Soon after its formation, in an effort to diversify its product line, Docutel hired Don Wetzel from IBM to head up a financial systems division. Wetzel's financial background led him to consider possible marketing opportunities in the banking field. He immediately focused on improving the relationship between consumers and Docutel's bank customers.

Not long before, while traveling in Europe, Wetzel had been struck by the emerging ATM technology he had seen there; cash-dispensing machines enabled customers to secure funds without having to go to a bank. Wetzel had the opportunity to observe a number of different machines, including ones developed by Chubb, De La Rue, and Cit/ Metior in England, France, Switzerland, and Sweden. Upon his return to the United States, convinced of their viability, he recommended that Docutel enter the cash dispenser field. Wetzel himself oversaw the production and design of the new machines, and the first unit was delivered in the last quarter of 1969. With its installation, the United States entered the era of electronic funds transfer (EFT) systems.

From its inception, the operation suffered from cash flow problems, owing primarily to higher than projected startup costs. The parent company was forced to sell Docutel to Information Processing Company, a Houston holding company specializing in computer software programs. But Docutel continued to push ahead with its cash-dispensing machines, and by the end of 1972, it had an estimated 1,250 units in operation, placing it in a dominant position in the young industry. But its efforts were attracting competition from firms such as Diebold, Mosler, and Burroughs, which had begun producing similar machines.

ATMs were the first widespread example of an EFT system. Initially, the EFT concept held two attractions for bankers. First, it was a new service for customers that made banking more convenient. Customers could visit the bank on evenings and weekends when bank offices were closed. ATMs also provided the services of an additional "teller" during peak weekday periods. Some bankers felt that such a service could give them a marketing advantage over their competitors, particularly during a period when Regulation Q forbade interest rate competition for deposits.

A second attraction was the cost savings. Presumably, human tellers could be replaced and ultimately even the number of checks could be reduced as customers made more of their transactions electronically. Unfortunately for the banks, the check reduction was never realized—credit cards could be substituted for cash, but EFT did not reduce the number of checks that were written. However, EFT substituted directly for checks in funds transfers, and more such substitution could be expected. A number of early ATMs used the bank's credit card, since a magnetic stripe could be encoded for use in the machines.

Encoding Standardization

When cash dispensers first appeared, they were activated primarily by credit cards that had a magnetic stripe on the back. While this procedure enabled banks to give their bank card customers the opportunity to use the machines, it did not offer access to customers who did not use their bank card. In late 1972, City National Bank of Columbus, Ohio, became the first bank in the nation to promote two cards—one a credit card and one a debit card for EFT. Its research showed that half its customers did not want to use BankAmericard in the ATMs, largely because they did not believe in using credit cards of any type. The research also showed that half its customers could not qualify for a credit card. A sizable proportion fell into both groups, but well over half of the bank's customers were still eliminated as potential credit cardholders.

City National's mass issuance of its new debit card produced a twelvefold increase in dollar volume on tellers and cash dispensers combined. The program received such widespread attention that the bank was deluged by visitors from all over the world who wanted to inspect its facilities. The bank's management was forced to institute a charge of $500 a visit in order to separate the serious visitors from the merely curious. Even that did not halt the flow.

Thrift institutions were also rapidly realizing that their future would be determined by their ability to enter the EFT era. If they did not develop their own systems, they were in danger of being frozen out by the banks, which viewed them as rivals. In the early 1970s, First Federal Savings and Loan of Lincoln, Nebraska, began its famous Hinky-Dinky system, which enabled savings account depositors to obtain funds in supermarkets and other "remote" locations.

Standardization is needed for any efficient exchange of information. For example, if checks are encoded differently by different banks, they cannot be processed by the same automated equipment throughout the country. The same principles apply to ATMs. A standardized magnetic encoding system allows a card to be used in many different machines in many different areas, which was a major short-term objective of industry leaders. Standardized encoding systems would enable manufacturers to standardize their machines and would allow the networking of machines made by different manufacturers.

Thus, the Joint On-line Communications and Specifications Committee set up by the thrift institutions cooperated with the ABA, Interbank, and BankAmericard to explore opportunities for on-line interchange of credit and transaction data. But the thrifts' efforts to be included in the future of EFT were opposed by the large commercial banks that controlled the bank card associations.

Mutual banks and S&Ls began working together to develop standard specifications for teller terminals in the late 1960s. Specifications were developed by the Mutual Institutions National Transfer System (MINTS). In the early 1970s, the U.S. Savings and Loan League pioneered negotiations with the T&E card companies; ultimately, those negotiations were turned over to MINTS.

Credit Card Companies Join the EFT Era

Debit cards were given a big boost when the Gerard Trust Bank in Philadelphia converted its American Express Gold card to a debit card. To convert the gold card to a debit card, American Express added a

Docutel stripe to the back of the card in the position of the third and fourth tracks, in addition to the regular ABA first and second tracks that were on all American Express cards.

Distributed through participating banks, American Express Gold cards could be used in cash dispensers; charges were debited immediately to the user's bank account. An additional feature was the ability to use the cards to obtain traveler's checks. American Express negotiated contracts for space in airports and other facilities convenient to travelers and began to place traveler's check dispensers around the country. The charges for transactions involving traveler's checks and cash advances did not appear on the cardholder's American Express bill but were handled through his or her bank account.

Initially, only American Express Gold cards could be used to activate bank cash dispensers, but both green and gold cards worked in the traveler's check dispensers. By November 1976, American Express had traveler's check dispensing units at sixteen airports across the United States, enabling cardholders to buy up to $500 worth of traveler's checks in $100 packages. All installations were on-line to American Express's Phoenix processing center where transactions were put on tape and sent to clearing banks, which made up paper checks that ended up at the customers' banks. There was no additional charge above the usual $1 charge for $100 worth of checks.

The test machines quickly proved successful, and American Express began to install them at airports across the country. To use the service, American Express cardholders had to apply for a personal identification number (PIN). Customers who encountered difficulties could use the phone attached to the dispenser to talk directly to the Phoenix processing center. Cardholders applying for a PIN signed a form authorizing American Express to debit their checking accounts at specified banks and attached a voided personal check to identify the location and account number.

The plan was inspired by a credit card survey showing that the service most sought after by traveling businesspeople was a convenient way to get funds away from home. Traveler's check dispensers were also seen to be a security advance over cash dispensers because of the two-step operation: a thief would have to first obtain the checks from the machine and then cash them.

In 1977, American Express began dispensing traveler's checks through bank ATMs that could also dispense cash, using IBM cash dispensers that could accommodate two different denominations of bills—a prime example of the speed with which the technology was changing during this period. That same year, following the successful installation of thirty-five dispensers in U.S. airports, American Express ordered thirty additional, specially designed machines to dispense traveler's checks.

By the fall of 1974, more than 2,500 cash dispensers and ATMs had been installed and about 2,700 more were on order, representing a total investment by depository institutions of over $210 million in hardware, software, and installation. Docutel continued to maintain its leadership in the manufacturing of automated banking equipment, with 2,050 cash dispenser and ATM installations, compared with less than 500 for all other domestic manufacturers. The basic price of its cash dispenser was about $17,000; an ATM cost about $30,000.

Although the number of ATMs in operation continued to grow, the public still appeared reluctant to embrace the new concept. By June 1976, ATM industry observer Linda Fenner Zimmer reported as part of her annual ATM directory that there were some 4,656 cash dispensers and ATMs installed in more than 1,000 financial institutions. A year later, the total had passed 6,000. Zimmer found, however, that the average number of transactions per installation per month was only 1,432, less than 15 percent of their capability. Low volume was a problem that would plague the industry until consumer acceptance became more widespread in the 1980s.

Success also continued to elude Docutel. In spite of its market leadership, Docutel showed little profitability. From its formation in 1967 until 1974, accumulated losses totaled $2.4 million; the losses largely stemmed from the startup years of 1968 to 1971. The company was briefly profitable in 1972 and 1973 but then fell back into the red, where it remained until the late 1970s. In 1979, the company posted a healthy net profit of $4.2 million. Three years later, it was acquired by Olivetti of Italy for $60 million. The following year, 1983, the company again changed hands when AT&T acquired 25 percent of Olivetti for $260 million with an option to increase its stake to 40 percent.

Despite the slow spread of customer acceptance, bank card companies continued to expand their ATM operations. Initially, both Visa and Master Charge had been content simply to affix a magnetic stripe to the back of their existing cards, enabling cardholders to access the ATMs. In fact, a large proportion of total transactions were made by consumers using bank credit cards. Problems caused by processing and customer confusion between the credit and debit functions of the cards inspired both Visa and Master Charge to develop a simple debit card.

In 1976, Visa launched its debit card, known as Entree. Soon after, Master Charge followed suit with its debit card known as Signet. While these cards were designed to be used like credit cards, banks treated the transactions as they would checks, by applying debits against deposit account balances rather than lines of credit. First National City Bank of Columbus was the first to adopt Visa's Entree card, and another fifty banks soon signed up. Master Charge's Signet card was much slower getting out of the gate, and limited adoptions by banks eventually prompted Master Charge to change the function of the card from debit to check guarantee.

ATM Fraud

Inevitably, as the use of ATMs expanded so did the number of cases of fraud. In 1975, according to an Interbank study of 815 ATMs operated by 125 important banks, the machines did a gross volume of $341 million from 10.5 million transactions. Fraud loss reported was $290,000, on 0.085 percent of volume. The available statistics (compiled by John Colin of the Chemical Bank of New York, which had been long involved with ATMs) showed that the most common fraud sources for ATMs were: (1) mailings of plastic cards and PIN numbers, (2) failure on the part of customers to keep cards and PINs separate, (3) punching the PIN into the machine when someone could observe it and copy the PIN, (4) duplication of magnetically encoded data by skimming, (5) violation of the transmission line to the ATM, (6) physical break-ins by force, (7) cracking the code of off-line installations, (8) breaches in security in card encoding departments, and (9) breaches in security with card manufacturers. Fraud exposure was not broken down in terms of dollar loss.

Apparently, the greatest problem facing owners of ATMs in 1977 was preventing field engineers from stealing cash from the machines. The second most serious problem arose from forged cards in departments within banks where custom encoding of cards was done by hand. A third similar problem was occurred in manufacturing plants where encoding was done before shipments were made.

With the increasing use of unattended banking machines in the late 1970s, there was a strong movement toward standardization of PINs. A method of encryption invented by IBM employees and adopted by the National Bureau of Standards (NBS) became the federal data encryption standard (DES), which was represented by the government as being adequate for all commercial applications, particularly EFT Systems. There were many critics of DES who felt that other encryption systems were more flexible, efficient, and secure. Because of the longer development time necessary for the other encryption systems, Interbank adopted DES in January 1978.

ATM Expansion in the Late 1970s

An article in the April 1977 issue of *BusinessWeek* declared that EFT systems were in the midst of a decline owing to consumer resistance, soaring costs, and legal snarls. This early postmortem proved premature, however. At that moment, Citibank was proceeding apace with its plan to install two full-service ATMs in most of its 270 branches by the end of 1977. Zimmer estimated that, by year's end, there had been 2,700 new installations of ATMs and cash dispensers—more than double the number installed in the previous year—bringing the total of operating ATMs and cash dispensers to about 8,000. Zimmer estimated average transaction volume to be about 2,000 per month per machine, excluding requests for balance information. However, some installations reported transaction totals of 10,000–15,000, and at least one averaged 27,000 per month. A small number of banks did charge a transaction fee but did not find the fee to be a serious deterrent to use.

At the end of 1977, Spencer Nilson estimated that there were more than twenty million debit cards in circulation, of which about fourteen million were in the United States. Outside of the United States, the Japanese had the greatest number, with 4.5 million, followed by Great Britain, with 1.25 million. No other country was estimated to have more than 158,000 debit cards.

In the late 1970s, implementation of EFT systems began in Switzerland, but in a slightly different mode from that developed in the United States. In 1976, the forty-two largest Swiss banks asked Electrowatt of Zurich to design and implement a cooperative network of ATMs for use by the end of 1979. Electrowatt chose the Dassault machine because its design was easily adapted to special requirements and offered the flexibility needed for upgrading to meet future customer needs. While recognizing the importance of communication with mainframe data files, the Swiss banks rejected the notion that the system had to be totally on-line. Instead, they chose a compromise "polling" system, which combined the economy of off-line operation with the security provided by periodic access to the mainframe through polling.

Each machine was designed to be polled once or twice an hour in the daytime; at night, the frequency was reduced to once every two hours. Daytime polling was scheduled to take about ten seconds; night-time polling was a bit lengthier. The total cost for the computer system was estimated to be a small fraction of what would be needed if each bank operated its own on-line system. The security disadvantages of a polled system were partially offset by a withdrawal limit on each machine of $100 per customer per day. Attempts to defraud the machine would show up within a single polling cycle.

As the popularity and use of ATMs finally began to spread rapidly in the late 1970s and early 1980s, banks began to search for ways to further accentuate their appeal. Additional utility could be provided if bank customers were allowed to access their account for cash even when they were outside of the bank's branch network.

The two major bank card companies had been preparing for nationwide networking for years. Their approaches, however, were vastly different. MasterCard announced a debit card called MasterCard II, for issue by cooperating banks to their customers. MasterCard II could be used only in specially marked ATMs throughout the country. Visa rejected the notion of a separate debit card, reasoning that two cards might stigmatize a credit card user as someone who lacked adequate balances to pay cash for purchases. A Visa card would function as both a credit and debit card, and presumably, only the user and the computer would know which type of transaction it was used for.

Unfortunately for both companies, the response of the larger banks to third-party debit cards was not overwhelming. For many reasons, including a strong desire to maintain their identity during a period of nationwide bank consolidation, banks began forming their own ATM network. Initially, local banks formed into regional networks, such as Yankee 24 in New England and NYCE in New York. Regional networks in turn joined the newly forming national network.

By 1982, there were six nationwide ATM networks existing or forming, with several others on the way. The six included the Plus System, begun by the Rocky Mountain Bank Card System under the direction of its president, Dale Browning; RIA (Regional Interchange Association); Exchange/ADP; Express Cash, offered by American Express; Cirrus, directed by Alex "Pete" Hart (who later became president of MasterCard) of the First Interstate Bancorporation; and Continet, a service offered by A. O. Smith Data Systems. Several more have sprung up in the past several years.

Despite the banks' initial reluctance, the bank card companies have also gained control of two networks. In 1988, MasterCard purchased the Cirrus network for $34 million, following in the footsteps of Visa, which had previously acquired the Plus network.

Networking facilitated the placement of ATMs at locations other than banks. Airports, train stations, gas stations, and gambling casinos were just a few of the sites chosen for ATMs. A number of employers allowed ATMs to be placed on their premises, helping to create an environment, in conjunction with expanded fringe benefits, in which their employees could receive nearly all financial services at work. Several banks also decided to automate former full-service branches.

To compete for the ATM customer, banks have begun to offer more attractive and sophisticated machines that use color, touch screens, and audio and video effects to help the customer conduct a wider array of banking functions, from deposits and withdrawals to transfers and even loans that are obtained as an advance on a credit card. All of this is done without any human intervention, which appeals to both our cultural bias toward do-it-yourself operations and our desire for privacy. If you do not have enough money in your account to make a withdrawal, a teller does not have to inform you of this embarrassing situation—the ATM simply returns your card.

ATM Use in the 1980s

By 1981, the United States had 38 percent of the world's ATMs, followed by Japan with 32 percent. The leading producer of ATMs in 1981 was NCR, with 11,240 units shipped. It was followed closely by Fujitsu of Japan, with 11,100 units, and then by Diebold, IBM, Docutel, and Omram of Japan, in that order. Most units installed in the United States in 1981 continued to be wall units on the outside of banks, accounting for 59 percent of total installations. Next were kiosk units with 18 percent, drive-up units with 10 percent, vestibule units with 7 percent, and lobby units with 6 percent. Expectations were that the number of wall units would decline as the other types expanded.

ATMs continued to proliferate throughout the 1980s. Zimmer estimated that by 1988 there were 81,681 ATMs installed in the United States alone—roughly one per thousand households. On a per household basis, the United States and Japan led all other countries in ATM installations. In Europe, Sweden had the highest ratio per household, although in total installations it trailed both England and France, which together accounted for more than half of all European ATM installations.

Although ATM installations continued throughout the decade, the strong upward trend flattened considerably around 1985 for a number of reasons, including banks' increasing concern about the costs of the systems. Having spent more than $2 billion on ATMs, banks began to wonder whether the systems were truly cost-justified. They noted that not only had total transaction volumes flattened out but adding more machines had diminished, not increased, the total number of transactions. Since it takes roughly two ATM transactions to displace one human teller transaction, Zimmer estimated that 8,000 transactions per month were needed to break even. However, the actual number of transactions per machine declined from a high of 7,200 per month in 1982 to just over 5,000 per month in 1987.

Banks have responded to this trend by charging ATM usage fees to their customers, reflecting the general trend among banks to make each service profitable. Presently, transaction fees for withdrawals average 25¢. Using a network such as Cirrus or Plus can cost a cardholder up to $1. Zimmer has reported that many banks are considering dropping per-transaction charges in favor of a flat annual fee ranging from $5 to $15.

In studying ATM problems, banks have found that the machines are heavily used by only about a third of bank customers. A 1987 survey carried out by the Center for Research and Development in Financial Services at the University of Connecticut found that only a third of Connecticut's residents felt that the offering of ATM services was very important in their choice of a bank. It is notable that this study was undertaken in the country's wealthiest state.

Older persons, who hold a significant portion of bank deposits, tend to be particularly reluctant to use ATMs. Future ATM growth is largely predicated upon the replacement of middle-aged and older persons with baby boomers who have grown up playing electronic games and hitting ATMs for cash.

The National Commission on Electronic Funds Transfer

The introduction of a sizable number of different approaches to electronic funds transfer in the early 1970s caused concern among consumers, who feared possible ill effects from the novel technology. As a result, their legislative representatives introduced a number of bills in Congress advocating a moratorium on EFT projects that affected consumers. In response, Congress set up the National Commission on Electronic Fund Transfers in 1974 to study the matter and recommend appropriate actions for the federal government. The commission, appointed by President Ford on 6 October 1975, was given two years to present its final report.

The work of the commission resulted in the Electronic Funds Transfer Act of 1978, which became effective on 8 February 1979. The act was in many ways reminiscent of the credit card legislation of a decade before in that it focused to a large extent on problems of distribution. The act did allow for the distribution of unsolicited debit cards, but only if they remained worthless until activated by the customer. Also mandated was sending disclosure of the customer's liability with the card, keeping a record of the phone number and address of a person to contact if the card was lost or stolen, and keeping other similar information available.

Although relatively little legislation resulted from the work of the commission, it did raise a large number of issues, ranging from privacy to industry concentration, and additional legislation was a possibility. Those who favored greater consumer privacy felt it was important to build in privacy protection during the initial phases of a new payment system. During commission hearings in the fall of 1976, Allen F. Westin, professor of public law and government at Columbia University, testified that, "unless Congress enacts a new national law to protect individuals whose personal records will be transferred electronically, individuals will have no way of defending themselves against violation of their personal privacy."

Professor Westin felt that when personal information is merged from a variety of sources to create a permanent financial database, a "trustee relationship" is created between the database manager and the individual account holder. The profile of an individual in the database would thus be a valuable legal property that should belong to the individual, not to the system. Those sharing Professor Westin's view would limit the use of such information to basic purposes for funds transfer and necessary monitoring for security, audit, and other protective processes.

Following the 1978 disbanding of the commission, two organizations were formed to promote the interests of companies engaging in EFT activities: the EFT Assocation in Washington, and the Electronic Money Council in Chicago; these organizations later merged in the fall of 1981.

Other EFT Applications

While ATMs have been the most valuable and most successful EFT systems developed, a number of others have also been tried, with varying degrees of success: check verification systems, automated gasoline and supermarket systems, telephone and computer sales and banking, and POS systems. POS systems hold the most promise for the near future, although they are still beset by numerous operational difficulties.

Check verification has been viewed by many as an interim move in the direction of the true electronic transfer of funds. One of the best-known check verification plans, Honest Face, was introduced by First National Bank of Atlanta on 4 October 1975. By 1977, all the supermarkets in Atlanta, and a large number of independent retailers had signed up for the plan and 465,000 cards had been distributed.

The Honest Face system used 380 AMCAT 1-C shopper-oriented POS terminals that had been designed by First National Bank for the program. A merchant's fee of 7.5¢ per check, plus a customer charge of $6.50 for bounced checks, which added up to about 9.5¢ per transaction, provided the revenue for the program. Unfortunately, the cost per transaction totaled 12.5¢, so the system did not break even. It was estimated that nineteen million transactions per year would be needed to achieve profitability. Honest Face was acquired by Telecredit in 1981 and then sold to Computers Plus in 1986 for approximately $3 million. Two years later, when Comdata acquired Computers Plus, the system became part of Comdata's Cashex division, which operates supermarket check-approval systems. Total revenues in 1988 were just under $4 million.

On the West Coast, Wells Fargo's Well Service check and credit authorization system generated profits soon after its inception in 1975, partly because of its simplicity. It utilized a simple keyboard unit that was similar to TRW's 4103, the most widely used authorization terminal in the world at that time, and generally regarded as the most trouble-free. In addition, Wells Fargo decided to do without the magnetic stripe, which it regarded as being too expensive and too difficult to use. By the summer of 1975, the bank had signed agreements with eighty-two merchants for an October pilot test involving 500 terminals. Well Service was a solid business operation, producing $60–$70 per month in merchant revenues for customer authorization in addition to a transaction charge of 4–7¢.

By the spring of 1977, Well Service had 1,000 terminal installations in California. Merchants were provided with instant access to the positive credit files of Western States Bank Card Association (Master Charge), NBI, American Express, Diners Club, Carte Blanche, and the negative files of TRW's Validata and Telecredit. In 1977, the merchant charge was $40 per month for each terminal, the transaction fee was 4–7¢, and there was an insurance fee covering checks drawn on California banks.

Spencer Nilson estimated that by the end of 1977 there were 44.82 million check guarantee cards in circulation worldwide, less than one-third of which were in the United States. Check guarantee plans included First National of Atlanta's Honest Face, Citibank's TransAction and Citicard, State Street of Boston's VEC, First of Boston's Money One, First of Chicago's Yes, Central Trust of Cincinnati's Owl, Security Pacific's Security Service, and large grocery store–owned check-approval systems. The world's largest check guarantee card was Eurocheque, the only multicountry check-cashing system. In 1977, there were 27.5 million Eurocheque cards in circulation, including eleven million in Great Britain.

Early in 1978, Chase Manhattan Bank joined Telecredit's Welcome Check Card Program, which allowed its checking account customers to have their checks accepted by merchants throughout the country who participated in Welcome Check. Their Chase Convenience Card contained Telecredit's Welcome Check symbol. An emergency cash feature also enabled them to obtain funds from participating banks. Welcome Check offered benefits to financial institutions that wished to offer their customers check guarantee services but did not want to maintain their own debit card. Many people expected Welcome Check to assume the dominant position in the United States, similar to that achieved by Eurocheque abroad.

Citibank ended its transaction check-cashing service in October 1978. The check guarantee plan had operated for three years and 700 merchants in the New York area had been signed up. However, of the 200,000 cards distributed to noncustomers, only 60,000 remained active. Citibank realized that check guarantee was, at best, a niche industry with a very limited application. It was suitable only for those businesses in which profit margins are too small to allow the use of credit cards, or customers lack such cards, or the average purchase is too high for routine use of cash. The supermarket was left as the primary arena for check cashing; charges were never very high, and store volume was significant enough to justify the cost of the machinery.

EFT Systems in the Gas and Retail Industries

In addition to its various applications in the bank industry, the new EFT technology was being adopted in other industries. In 1971, after the success of the early pump-it-yourself pilot programs, the oil companies developed card-activated pumps. The initial purpose of the pumps was to allow customers to handle the entire gasoline transaction themselves. Some believed that business could be generated in a number of new ways: stations could be installed where there were currently no stations or where space was either limited or at a premium; service hours could be extended well after closing; security could be improved by the elimination of the need for cash on the premises. The pumps could also provide supplemental self-service to existing high-traffic locations. For a variety of reasons, full automation did not develop, and semiautomation became the norm in retail gasoline distribution.

By January 1973, automatic gasoline vending via plastic cards was a reality, thanks to a process invented by Revenue Systems Ltd. Later that year, Docutel and Atlantic Richfield joined together to test card-activated self-service gas stations. When a customer inserted the Atlantic Richfield card into the console, a panel lighted up and said, "Please wait—Remove card when returned." During the waiting period of about eight seconds, an on-line credit check was made to National Data Corporation of Atlanta. Card identification was done with North American Rockwell's optical character reader. If approved, the card was returned and the instruction panel changed to "Press pump—Select button." To protect the customer from forgetting to take out the card, a beeper sounded if it was not removed in fifteen seconds. Also, the pump would not turn on until the card was removed.

The customer selected the type of gasoline by pressing one of six buttons on an adjacent panel. The buttons indicated whether the fuel type was available and whether the pump was in use. After the customer completed fueling, a receipt was printed showing the amount and type of fuel purchased, the price per gallon, the date and time of day the pump was used, the refund due (if any), and the station identification number. The complete transaction took an average of three and a half minutes. If the amount of gasoline received was less than what the cash inserted had paid for, a printed receipt showed the difference and the console instructed the customer to see the attendant for a refund. The machine would also accept dollar bills.

Customers using BankAmericard and Master Charge cards had to first go to the attendant to obtain a "cash card" issued in even-dollar amounts. The terminal was designed to retain cards identified by National Data as invalid and to reject those that were expired. At that time, in 1973, the maximum amount for a single transaction was $12.

Atlantic Richfield's agreement with Docutel involved a commitment to fifteen installments in 1973. The Docutel system, which could control an eighteen-pump installation, cost about $31,000. A six-pump system cost about $16,000. Mobil, Phillips, Continental, Standard Oil of Indiana, and Humble all experimented with Docutel systems.

During the energy crisis of 1973–74, the trial of card-activated, automatic gas-dispensing systems continued to move forward. A new wrinkle was added when City National of Columbus, Ohio, led by the innovative John Fisher, put ATMs in self-service gas stations. The U.S. comptroller of the currency approved two applications from City National to open its Gas-N-Go stations, which were staffed by human tellers and one automatic teller and were located on former station lots that were converted to self-service. While Gas-N-Go did not at first have card-activated gas pumps, it was anticipated that they would be added later.

City National was not the only bank that combined gasoline distribution and electronic funds transfer. Central Trust of Canton, Ohio, had a pilot operation as well. In California, Citibank's Transaction Technology used 12,000 Magic Middle cards (see Chapter 10) at U.S.A. Petroleum stations, dispensing gasoline from nine dual-dispenser Tokheim and Bennett pumps.

By 1978, five years after the installation of the first one, there were still only 1,500 card-activated pumps in service in the United States—less than one percent of the 190,000 self-service pumps of all kinds. They were slow to catch on for several reasons. First, they were expensive: the price per pump for card-activated systems ran about $4,000, not including the high installation costs, compared with $1,000–1,500 for regular pumps, many of which were nearly indestructible. Second, card-activated systems were most efficient when operated as satellites under centralized control, but the oil companies in the late 1970s were divesting themselves of company-owned stations to save capital. Third, the credit card plans in general were so unprofitable for the oil companies that there was pressure to turn the credit function over to the bank cards, which were achieving greater market penetration.

Perhaps the major barrier to card-activated pumps was the existence of laws in nearly every state prohibiting unattended retail gasoline sales, partly to prevent the purchase of gasoline by children. As a result, nonretail use of card-activated gasoline systems became somewhat more important. By 1978, at least twenty wholesalers operated completely unattended facilities using card-activated pumps at remote locations.

In Corpus Christi, Texas, Susser Petroleum's Save-A-Dollar Clubs of America were begun in 1975. Club members could purchase gasoline at sixteen unattended locations in the Corpus Christi area. Over 35,000 Save-A-Dollar gasoline cards were issued to Corpus Christi residents who were approved for membership after screening. The cards allowed them to activate self-service dispensing units twenty-four hours a day at seven retail locations linked to an IBM System-7 computer that handled the paperwork on each transaction. From the time a customer inserted the card in a pump until the time a bill was received, no human intervention was needed. Susser claimed that the system enabled it to charge 2¢ less per gallon than the average charge of other vendors in the area.

A similar service was later operated by the A. R. Wright Company in 1984. Issuing its own credit card under the name Wright Express, the company operated a totally unattended twenty-four-hour station in Portland, Maine. The card was distributed to fleet operators who preferred the limited use of the cards to the bank and oil company cards, which could be abused, often in cooperation with an employee.

At least three tests using Docutel equipment were discontinued by 1978. Standard Oil of Indiana had experimented at two locations in Milwaukee since 1976, Atlantic Richfield had run an elaborate test in Los Angeles, and Shell had tested Citibank cards in Houston. At the other extreme, in Sweden, where unattended pumps were legal, fully one-fifth of the country's gasoline was sold from self-service pumps using 2,500 Audac and Asea note acceptors.

Japan's Unmanned Supermarket

Another less successful attempt to adopt EFT technology was the Japanese experiment with unmanned supermarkets in the mid-1970s. Japan's O.K. supermarket chain devoted one-third of a store to testing a computerized, automat-type vending system that had been developed by the Japanese government during the previous five years at a cost of more than $1.5 million. The store had sixty-seven vending machines (some refrigerated) displaying 3,000 items. Customers obtained items by inserting magnetic cards and punching selector switches. A computer recorded the sales and released the door locks. The products were removed by hand by customers and placed in shopping carts.

One cashier was stationed at the checkout counter, where magnetic cards were inserted into a special cash register that printed an instant, itemized sales slip. The computer also determined what items had to be restocked. Checkout time for customers was about seven times faster than in conventional stores. In mass-production, the computerized vending system was estimated to cost around $340,000, including installation costs.

Despite the system's smooth performance, Japanese customers reacted negatively. Daily sales were only about 12 percent of those expected, even though prices were approximately 7 percent lower than in other markets. A second test of the automated supermarket carried out in the Yaohan Department Store in Atami City was far more successful. The Atami version was smaller than the O.K. supermarket version, with only half the number of vending units. However, the smaller system generated about ten times the daily volume of the first system. Contributing to the success of the Atami system may have been the fact that it was open twenty-four hours a day and was located in one of the most popular hot springs resorts in Japan. It was run by only six people on three shifts using only one register.

Telephone Applications: Home Banking

Although ATMs grew steadily throughout the 1970s, the development of other EFT systems was not as smooth. Telephone bill payment by EFT, for example, did not show the promise originally projected until very late in the decade. The first such program, designed by Howard Philips and his Telephone Computing Services Company, was begun by Seattle-First National Bank in the fall of 1973. Known as Dial-A-Computer, it was promoted as the answer to many personal record-keeping needs, including family bookkeeping, bill payments, appointment scheduling, and even math problems, solved by a personal calculator. A printout mailed to subscribers every two weeks summarized expenditures for the month and the year to date and gave considerable additional information.

The cost of the hookup to the subscriber's home was $6.50 per month. Subscribers were assigned a code number that gave them access to 100 units of computer time per month, activated by a touch-tone telephone in their home. The difficulty was in marketing these diverse services. Only a handful of the bank's customers subscribed, and few of those felt it was of any value. After six months of operation, the service was discontinued.

Although the Dial-A-Computer telephone transfer system failed in Seattle after only six months, Telephone Computing Services Company kept modifying and promoting its basic idea. By 1977, the company had installed thirteen of the twenty-five telephone transfer systems in use across the country and had contracted with an additional sixty banks to develop Telephone Computing Service's Pay-By-Phone service if they decided to proceed with the plan.

While Dial-A-Computer was a package service that included a calculator, a personal reminder calendar of events, income tax data collection and preparation, familly budgeting, and checkless bill payment, Pay-By-Phone offered only the bill payment service. (Philips, who had founded Telephone Computing Services in 1971, restructured his original package service after market research showed that only the checkless bill payment service was marketable.) In addition, it was marketed to banks rather than individuals. The banks then sold the service to their customers as a special banking service to enhance their checking and savings accounts. Contracts specified a one-time charge to participating banks of $40,000–500,000, plus a transaction royalty of half a cent to Telephone Computing Services. The company offered a variety of software to the banks to fit local marketing requirements.

An important event in the field of credit card authorization was the development of the transaction telephone. First placed on the market in

April 1975, the terminal was designed and developed by AT&T in a joint effort with BancSystems, one of fifteen interbank associations. While the transaction telephone had many other functions, it enabled the customer to verify bank account balances by sliding the magnetically encoded card through a slot in the telephone, inserting his or her PIN through the touch-tone dial, and receiving the information audibly. An automatic dialer enabled the merchant to access many different data banks. A green or red light could indicate approval or disapproval of the transaction.

The major advantages offered by this transaction telephone were the reliability of the manufacturer and the compatibility of AT&T's products with the phone system. An added bonus was the low monthly charge, which was expected to be $20–25 per month, making the transaction telephone well suited to the needs of the large number of low-volume merchants with fewer than 300 credit transactions per month. The system became widely used in the 1980s for credit card verification. However, it has yet to catch on as a debit system.

A new element was added to EFT systems when Bank One of Columbus, Ohio, began its home-banking experiment in 1980. Designed by John Fisher and John Russell, two of the most innovative bankers involved in the development of EFT, the project evolved over some five years of experience with interactive television. In 1975, Fisher and Russell had witnessed the introduction of a two-way cable system called Qube by Warner Communications. They were impressed by the system's potential, but they soon decided that the slow growth of two-way cable systems nationally would impede the development of home banking. Therefore, they were inclined toward a system that used the telephone for interactive communication between the customer and the bank's computer.

Home banking represented an advance over telephone bill payment systems: the user could see the transaction information on a screen, and it was no longer necessary to mail paper statements to customers. The video electronics method was faster than the audio method used for telephone bill payment; several items could be transferred to the screen in the time that it took to hear a single piece of information spoken over the telehone. Another advantage was that the computer terminal–based home-banking program could be used to obtain other nonbanking-related types of information, a feature that was useful in marketing the system. Individuals and businesses that acquired computer terminals or personal computers for other reasons were a ready market for home banking.

Fisher and Russell decided to use the Viewdata system, which had been developed by the British Postal Service. Called Channel 2000, the project was started as a joint effort between Bank One and a library services company called OCLC. Following Bank One's experiment, a number of other similar experiments were begun elsewhere in the country. In San Diego, Mission Cable TV, a wholly owned subsidiary of Cox Cable Communications of Atlanta, invited banks in California to participate in a joint experiment. Accepting the offer were Security Pacific, United California Bank, and California First Bank. Yet another experiment was begun in Knoxville, Tennessee, where United American Service Corporation and United American Bank formed a joint home-banking venture with CompuServe Corp and Radio Shack.

Point-of-Sale Systems

By the late 1980s, the proportion of credit card users who paid in full each month, using only the issuer's "free" credit, remained at about 50 percent, the same percentage that it had been in 1970. Elimination of these "free riders" has been a driving force behind the use of debit cards at point-of-sale (POS) machines.

A debit card is one that debits the account of the user when funds are withdrawn or expended. The most common example is the card used at an ATM. A POS machine is similar to an ATM in that it reads a magnetic stripe on the card and requires the user to input his or her PIN. However, instead of dispensing cash, the POS machine merely authorizes the transaction, debiting funds from the cardholder's account and crediting them to the merchant.

Three businesses are connected by a bank-affiliated POS system. When the customer hands the debit card to the merchant and enters his or her PIN, the information travels over leased or dial-up telephone lines to the merchant's bank, and then to a switching company that is on-line to other banks. If there are sufficient funds, they are transferred from the customer's account to the merchant's account at the merchant's bank. If funds are insufficient, the merchant is notified to halt the transaction.

Today, for a number of reasons, very few transactions are made at POS terminals with debit cards. First, there is no agreement among banks, retailers, and switching companies as to who will pay for the service, which involves high telecommunications charges. Consumers will not pay and are otherwise resistant to a card that would eliminate what they regard as the "free float" offered by the credit card. Even though debit card POS transactions grew by 52 percent in 1988, they and other electronic payment means together were used by only about 2 percent of customers.

The major impediment to large-scale POS systems has been the fantastic cost of having every merchant and every bank in the country (and ultimately the world) on-line at all times. The two proposed solutions involve the smart card, which allows funds to be debited internally, and batch processing (generally daily) of the transactions, facilitated by the automated clearinghouse (ACH). The latter, which allows for the use of automatic payroll deposits and automatic bill payment, is a batch-process transfer network among banks that has been in place for many years.

At the 1988 Electronic Funds Transfer Association Expo held in Washington D.C., members were split on the benefits of on-line networks versus ACHs for debit card transactions. In lieu of industry consensus, a number of merchants and banks began using POS systems. In April 1985, InterLink, a POS network involving the five biggest commercial banks in California, became operational. Each bank was responsible for enlising merchants for the network. As expected, the system was most attractive to merchants that had traditionally not accepted credit cards, such as supermarkets, gas stations, and convenience stores. Convenience stores find the system attractive because it generates higher average sales than cash does; they also like the guaranteed payment versus the uncertainty of a check.

There can be little doubt that EFT systems have become an integral part of many people's lives. The ubiquitous ATMs can be found in even the most remote parts of the United States and Europe. Many people now do their banking without any interaction with human tellers, transferring funds from one account to another, making balance inquiries, payments, and withdrawals, all electronically. However, EFT systems have yet to make the credit card obsolete, as many have predicted. Aside from ATMs and cash dispensers, only POS systems hold out any promise for the near future. Other EFT applications remain uncertain—more hype and possibility than profitable reality. Nevertheless, as the technology improves, EFT systems will certainly play a significant role in our move toward totally paperless banking.

10

The Changing Face of the Credit Card

A HISTORY OF THE CREDIT CARD INDUS-
try would hardly be complete without chronicling the development of
the credit card itself. Over the years, it has taken many forms: the dog-
tag-like charga-plates of the retail industry, the paper cards of the gas
industry, and the sophisticated plastic cards of today with their various
magnetically encoded stripes. From its very inception, the primary function of the credit card, and later the debit card, has been identification.
The card identified the bearer as the legitimate owner of a particular
credit line or bank account and authorized the merchant to accept that
person's credit or assets as payment.

The card has changed shape for various reasons. Some alterations
have been made to take advantage of new technology, such as the magnetic stripe. Most, however, have been the result of attempts to make
the cards more secure. Previous chapters have demonstrated that the
history of credit card misuse or fraud is nearly as old as the industry.
Given the vulnerabilities of the system, a thief has rarely had to learn
the arts of printing and engraving to create spending power. A lost,
stolen, or counterfeit credit card is as good as cash and often far more
difficult to detect than bogus currency.

The problem has been that any security methodology is con-
strained by considerations of cost and difficulty of use by the cardholder
or merchant, which were prime considerations with the tremendous
proliferation of credit cards during the 1970s. Any technique that would

greatly increase the cost of producing the billions of cards needed by the industry—such as putting the owner's picture on the card—was out of the question. Also undesirable were procedures that would destroy the spontaneity of the transaction, since that could result in the loss of impulse sales, which are so important to so many merchants.

One commonly used method of identification, a signature on the back of the card, relies on the ability of the clerk handling the transaction to recognize a forged signature by comparing the signature on the slip with that on the card. This method of identification was and continues to be vulnerable to forged signatures made by professionals on the card backs.

Another popular method of proving identity has been to request additional pieces of identification, such as a driver's license. The weaknesses of this commonsense method are twofold: thieves can easily fabricate identification to match the stolen card, and the demand for additional identification has proven to be both time-consuming and annoying for the customer. Another idea that the credit card companies have experimented with is the personal identification number (PIN), which can be checked through a computer that matches it to the card number. The development of the PIN proved particularly useful in the ATM industry.

Picture Cards

The driving force behind the "face" card, which is a plastic card with a photograph of the owner's face, has been the Polaroid Corporation. Polaroid began actively promoting face cards, or picture cards, in the 1960s as a way of developing the commercial potential of its instant photography. Although tests showed the face card to be very useful in reducing fraud, a congressional investigation of the fraudulent use of cards demonstrated its flaw: it was relatively easy to remove the photograph and substitute another, presumably of the credit card thief.

Another difficulty with the face card was that it was expensive. Compared with a basic material cost of 15¢ for a mass-produced conventional card in 1970, the face card cost approximately 40 cents. On the positive side, however, picture cards were seen by many banks as a desirable marketing feature for customers. Some banks began offering them as an option, while others made it mandatory for cardholders.

All face cards had the picture on the back, which presented difficulties because many clerks would not turn the card over to see whether there was a picture there. Apparently, pictures were not placed on the front because neither BankAmericard nor Master Charge wanted attention taken from their logo.

In June 1970, Polaroid executives testifying before the House of Representatives estimated that two million picture cards were in use, representing 4 percent of total bank cards outstanding. At that time, Polaroid claimed that no one had yet succeeded in fraudulently using this card. By mid-1973, however, only 600 out of 13,000 banks nationwide—less than 5 percent—were issuing picture cards.

One reason the picture cards were not widely used was that the Polaroid card, which accounted for more than 90 percent of all bank picture cards, was a "soft" card: the photograph was inserted into a plastic pouch through a slit in the side and heat-sealed; the picture could be replaced by simply slitting open the side of the pouch. In 1972, in an attempt to eliminate the problem, Polaroid introduced its ID-3 hard-card technique: the photograph was impregnated with plastic after being attached to the card. Called the PolaPress system, it took only two and a half minutes from the time a customer sat down for the photo until he or she was handed a finished card ready for use. At that time, the unit cost per card was 50–55¢, including the plastic, photographic film, magnetic stripe, and embossing foil.

Another major drawback with picture card identification was that the cardholder would have to be present for a photograph to be taken each time the card was reissued, which was theoretically possible for banks but not feasible for T&E card companies, since cardholders seldom entered their offices. Other methods of identification ran into civil rights objections. Those concerned with privacy objected to the use of fingerprints, palm prints, and voice prints for identification. The use of driver's licenses for identification was given a setback in 1976 with the release of a study by the American Bankers Association (ABA) indicating that 51 percent of all fraud cases in opening new checking and savings accounts involved false licenses.

Magnetic Stripe

A particularly important addition to the credit card was the magnetic stripe, which was first developed by IBM in the mid to late 1960s. Initially, it was used in conjunction with American Airlines and American Express for ticket vendoring at O'Hare Airport in Chicago. The magnetic stripe was particularly suited for use in the credit card industry because it was the least costly method of storing digital information on a credit card. Information is stored on a magnetic tape, similar to that used in a tape recorder, in binary form (ones and zeros). When the stripe is passed over a head, the information is read and interpreted by the processor.

For many years, there was no widespread agreement on the use of the magnetic stripe for reading credit cards by machine. By late 1972, although magnetic stripe technology was workable and in use in some places, there was some disagreement about whether it was the best way to read credit cards. In the fall of 1972, Dee Hock, president of NBI, stated that his firm was concentrating on magnetic encoding and recommended that banks look at it seriously. At that time, even the top administration at Bank of America was not fully behind magnetic stripe technology. At the competing Interbank, it was reported that some of the largest member associations were strongly in favor of a different technology that read embossed characters. Field tests had already shown this method to be more economical and trouble-free, as well as more likely than any application of the magnetic stripe to discourage fraud.

A major controversy arose toward the end of 1972 concerning the third track on the card. The first track had been taken by the International Air Transport Association (IATA), while the second track followed the format set by the ABA. The second track was read for identification when a card was put into an ATM. It was generally recognized that the third track would be a "read-write" track that would enable current information, such as an account balance, to be first read by the machine and then replaced with the new balance after a transaction had been made. The third track was considered particularly necessary for the off-line operation of ATMs.

The major parties concerned appeared to be cooperating on creating the standards necessary for the third track. As mentioned in Chapter 9, the Joint On-line Communications and Specifications Committee of the thrift institutions cooperated with the ABA, Interbank, and BankAmericard. Opposing the standaridzed third track, however, was Docutel, which did not want to alter the character of its encoding technique to conform to the new standards. IBM also did not believe that a third track was necessary, since it felt that all units should be on-line.

In early 1973, Docutel bowed to the pressure from other industry members and indicated that if the thrift institutions' proposal for standardization of the third track was universally adopted by other manufacturers, Docutel would have no choice but to go along with it. It was estimated that, by April 1973, more than thirty-one million plastic cards were in circulation with some form of visible or invisible magnetic encoding to make them machine-readable. Approximately 85 percent of all cards used a magnetic stripe to store both permanent and changeable data on the back. About one-half of those magnetic stripes were on bank, T&E, and airline credit cards.

Citibank's Magic Middle

In spite of the substantial number of cards being produced, it became apparent that magnetic encoding on credit cards left the system extremely vulnerable to massive fraud. Among the major holdouts against the magnetic stripe were the National Retail Merchants Association (NRMA), many major retailers, Diners Club, and Carte Blanche. Many observers felt that the magnetic stripe had been widely accepted in the credit card industry largely as the result of the bank card industry's ultimate objective of transforming its credit cards into vehicles for electronic funds transfer and credit authorization.

A special task force on bank card standardization among ABA members recommended adoption of a rigid magnetic stripe standard in its report published in January 1971. The first track, reserved for IATA, had a density of 210 bits per inch, which was required for storing enough information to issue tickets and make reservations. The second track, the ABA track, had a lower density of seventy-five bits per inch— enough to store a cardholder's account number, expiration date, and other optional information. The lower bit density of the second track was a compromise, theoretically enabling the bank card to be used at the unsophisticated merchant level. The computer tapes that generally contained 800 or 1,600 bits per inch could only be operated in air-conditioned, static, and dust-free rooms.

The reduction of the bit density on the magnetic stripe made it easier to decipher and copy and, therefore, made the cards more subject to fraud. One of the organizations most seriously concerned with the vulnerability of the magnetic stripe was the nation's second-largest bank, First National City Bank of New York, or Citibank. To uncover and demonstrate the inherent flaws in the magnetic stripe then in use, Citibank in 1973 set up a contest involving students at the California Institute of Technology, administered through Citibank's California subsidiary, Transaction Technology.

The ground rules of the contest were quite simple. The company wanted to find out if it was possible for people with a minimal knowledge to come up with effective means of defrauding the magnetic stripe system. A total of $15,000 in prize money was offered to students who could come up with effective techniques to defraud the magnetic stripe system. Students who entered the contest were given a written statement on the magnetic stripe, a twenty-three-page compilation of credit card and magnetic stripe specifications, and a list of technical documents on the subject that were readily available from outside sources. Contestants were given sixty days to produce an operational device or technique; at the end of that period, they were given an hour with company executives to present their technique and explain the principle upon which it was based.

An awards dinner was held in Pasadena, California, on 29 March; checks totaling $15,000 were handed out to twenty-two teams comprising thirty students. (The first prize was $5,000.) The top awards went to techniques and devices that were the most elementary, that used materials commonly available to anyone. Points were also awarded to devices that could most easily be constructed and operated by persons who had little or no knowledge of electronics or mechanical aptitude. The first-prize winner came up with a technique that could be explained by word of mouth in less than two minutes and required less than $5 for equipment. He used an iron laid over the original tape to make a duplicate magnetic tape, which could then be glued onto the card.

In the fall of 1973, the reason for Citibank's demonstration of the drawbacks of the magnetic stripe became apparent. Beginning with check authorization cards, Citibank introduced its new encoding technique known as the Magic Middle. Instead of utilizing a magnetic stripe, which can be easily copied and transferred to another card, Citibank's Magic Middle encoded information in the card itself through a series of holes. The terminal that would read these cards was relatively inexpensive and utilized a light source and a photosensitive leader at the other end. The rationale behind Magic Middle cards was that while the pattern of holes could be duplicated, the process of duplicating the pattern would be so time-consuming and capital-intensive that it was not likely to be done. The magnetic stripe, on the other hand, could be copied to another card in a matter of a few seconds, allowing the perpetrator of the fraud to return the original card to the user.

The card was developed by Transaction Technology, which had been set up in Cambridge, Massachusetts, for the purpose of developing magnetic stripe technology. (The company was later moved to Santa Monica, California, and put under the control of Jack Scantlin, who developed the Magic Middle technology.) By the time Citibank began to make the Magic Middle cards operational, its investment in them had been estimated at more than $20 million.

Citibank originally used its new encoding technology on 750,000 cards for check cashing only. It was then adapted for use with all 1.2

million Master Charge accounts for credit authorization. It also allowed Citibank customers to access data on their checking accounts. Citibank came under severe criticism from other credit card and banking officials for not joining the industry in a united front to back the ABA-endorsed magnetic stripe. However, Citibank did have the largest operational credit authorization system of any commercial bank in the world. Shortly after Citibank acquired Carte Blanche, the Magic Middle technology was added to those cards as well. In 1978, John Reed of Citibank projected that there would be twenty-five million Magic Middle cards in circulation internationally by 1983.

In late 1975, another magnetic stripe controversy emerged. Many of the world's largest manufacturers of banking equipment were designing their machines to rewrite the third track at 210 bits per inch with each transaction. Herman Ziegler of IBM felt that such density was not possible on a large scale. The machines' inability to read and write at such high levels of density was compounded by the lack of an industrywide test center to guarantee tolerance limits of adopted standards for hardware manufacturers in the industry.

By the end of 1978, most of the controversy over the magnetic stripe appeared to be diminishing. The limitations on magnetic stripe encoding were becoming fairly well recognized, and alternatives such as optical character recognition (OCR) were being looked at very seriously. The magnetic stripe was rejected for use on passports by the International Civil Aviation Organization (ICAO) and the International Association of Passport Officials based in Toronto. By this time, magnetic stripe encoding was seen as merely a backup technology to OCR encoding. Citibank had proven that magnetic encoding was neither desirable nor necessary, having brought its electronic banking network to an enviable level of volume and efficiency with a random, prefabricated, unchangeable, unduplicatable code built into the card.

In the summer of 1979, the controversy over the magnetic stripe was reactivated by Dee Hock's announcement that all Visa cards issued after 1 April 1980 would have to have the magnetic stripe on the back. Visa's action was thought to be an attempt to force Citibank into adopting the magnetic encoding technology it had always repudiated.

The ABA adopted the magnetic stripe as a standard for the banking industry in 1971 because it had characteristics needed for off-line applications, including the ability to store changeable data in a read/write mode. However, EFT, particularly as it developed in the United States, went on-line rather than off-line, permitting storage of transaction data in the mainframe of the computer where it was relatively safe, not on the card where it could be altered.

Citibank became somewhat vulnerable when nationwide ATM networks began to form in 1982; its machines were not compatible with the ATMs of other banks. There are several possible reasons why the Magic Middle card did not catch on nationally. First, it challenged an existing and widely used technology; to replace that technology would have required significant retooling of ATMs as well as card processors. Secondly, it could be used for identification purposes only and was not suitable for a read-write environment without a magnetic stripe added to it. Finally, it would have given Citibank an enormous advantage over the other banks, a situation Citibank's competitors would not have willingly accepted.

Optical Character Recognition

In the late 1970s, when it became apparent that EFT would not make much of a dent in the number of credit card sales slips that had to be processed, attention turned again to more efficient means of handling the paper.

To cope with the rapidly increasing flood of paper more quickly, accurately, and less expensively, the optical character recognition technology appeared to be most feasible. OCR had been around for a long time in many forms and had been used successfully for high-speed reading of checks, currency, coupons, and documents of all shapes and sizes.

Oil companies had been successful in using OCR effectively for credit card sales slips processed under controlled conditions not possible with bank and T&E cards. In the late 1970s, eight of the thirteen largest processing organizations (excluding oil companies) also used OCR, but each of those installations was unique in its determination of what items to process through the methodology. However, OCR had been incorporated into new optical scanners designed for high-speed reading of partially encoded credit card sales slips, making it possible for processors to handle as few as two million accounts annually and still benefit from OCR use.

The use of OCR to process credit card business had been developed to a high state of efficiency by Recognition Equipment Inc. for fifteen of the major oil companies in the United States and Canada, using Trace equipment, which was originally developed for high-speed processing of magnetically encoded checks. But oil companies had been able to obtain acceptance levels as high as 80 to 95 percent only because they had the ability to control inspection and maintenance of the imprinters used in gas stations selling their products. Banks and T&E companies could not maintain that degree of control with independent merchants.

It was also recognized that even if EFT systems at the point of sale were widely implemented, it would affect only about 5 percent of all establishments honoring credit cards, and not much more than 20 percent of total volume, owing to the cost involved. OCR technology was the only way to improve efficiency over the ensuing decade.

While the credit card industry debated the effectiveness of OCR, it had already been successfully adopted by numerous supermarkets across the country. Supermarkets encoded all items with the universal product code (UPC), which is read by a wand. Starting with six UPC installations in 1974, the number jumped to forty-two in 1975, 103 in 1976, and 201 by the end of 1977. Since the supermarket industry was committed to the UPC, it was reasonable to assume that any card honored by supermarkets had to be wand-readable.

Retail stores were committed to the OCR-A font, which they were beginning in 1978 to add to all of their cards for wand-reading. American credit card companies were prompted to think about adding OCR as the Germans had done—to make their cards compatible with the requirements of the grocery and retail merchants.

As the 1970s ended, it appeared that OCR was winning out over magnetic encoding as the preferred machine-readable technology. Magnetic impulses could too easily be altered; in addition, the magnetic stripe could not be read by the card bearer. Retailers, backed by a decision of the NRMA, moved full speed ahead toward the implementation of OCR-A and were soon reading merchandise tags as well as their own credit cards through this method.

In late 1978, OCR was given another boost at the expense of magnetic encoding when the ICAO and the International Association of Passport Officials agreed that there was no practical and economically justifiable way of allowing custom officials to detect and verify magnetic data on passports. At that time, Germany favored OCR-B, the United States favored OCR-A, and Canada had not decided between A and B. Finally, the decision by Visa in 1982 to offer all three modes—magnetic stripe, UPC, and OCR—on its electron Visa cards made it apparent that the varying modes were here to stay.

The electron Visa card provided by itself a short course in all of the major developments in credit card technology of the late 1970s and early 1980s. Alarmed by the success of the ATM networks, Visa had produced a card that was compatible with ATMs and POS machines of all types. Not only did the new card have the banking industry's magnetic stripe, but it also had the retail industry's OCR standard and the supermarkets' UPC code. The new card displayed the logo *e*, the international symbol for electron, and the raised lettering that had been on credit and debit cards since the charga-plate days had been eliminated. An attractive feature of the electron Visa card was that grocers and retailers who had nonmagnetic authorization equipment could access the information on it and would not have to invest in magnetic stripe–compatible equipment.

Smart Cards

As with any rapidly developing industry, not every effort has been successful. One such effort was an attempt to produce a card that could be used to transfer funds from the buyer to the seller at the point of sale. The success of cash dispensers and ATMs in the late 1970s represented only a small victory to the true adherents of paperless banking. With few exceptions, debit card transactions were made on bank premises, saving some teller time perhaps, but doing little to stem the flow of checks that kept increasing at about a 7 percent annual rate. Attempts to introduce debit cards at the point of sale were not very successful primarily because of the absence of a mechanism for transferring funds from the buyer to the seller.

While devices existed that used telephone lines to authorize and facilitate such transactions, they were costly and cumbersome and each device required a dedicated phone line. Initially, using the third track of the card to store balances was a possibility. A buyer could go to a store with a $300 balance on the third track of his or her card, purchase an item for $100, and have the balance on the track rewritten to $200. All of this would be off-line so that a dedicated phone line would not be necessary.

Unfortunately, a number of clever ways were found to read and alter the third track, making it simple to "counterfeit" electronic currency. In addition, to use an off-line debit card, the owner's PIN had to also be encoded on the card so that the POS machine could read the number and see whether it matched the PIN given by the presumed owner of the card. However, this necessitated the use of a decoding algorithm that was eventually deciphered and used with stolen cards whose third track could be read.

These potential problems, in conjunction with their EFT technology, which did rely upon on-line systems, caused some Europeans to take a different approach. They decided to store both the PIN and balance information in a computer chip embedded in the card. Since a chip can carry several thousand items of information, it offers far greater possibilities for encrypting identifying information than does the magnetic stripe and is thus much more difficult to decode and defeat.

The first patents on the chip card, or "smart" card, date back to 1968 when Juergen Dethloff and Helmut Groettrup of West Germany filed for a patent on a method to protect chip information from imitation or counterfeiting. In 1970, Ellingbol of TRW in the United States filed for a patent on "active electrical components [microelectronic circuits] in a card with bevelled edges." However, the major push to promote the smart cards came from the French. Three large French companies, Honeywell-Bull, Flonic Schlumberger, and Philips, invested heavily in smart card technology and were aided in the development of the Carte à Memoire by the French Government. With the election of the Mitterrand government in 1981, official aid was discontinued and much of the research and development work on the smart card ceased. Mitterrand's nationalization of major French industries (including the banks) and his curtailment of funds for noncritical projects resulted in financial cutbacks that stifled smart card development in France.

Smart card development did continue after the French government stopped its aid, but at a much slower rate because of technological obstacles as well as the worldwide recession in the early 1980s, which slowed up R&D of all types in most Western countries. One of the most severe technological obstacles was the card thickness that was needed to house and protect the chip. Such thickness made the card difficult to fit into most wallets, which made it unappealing to consumers.

Despite cutbacks in funding, France retained its leadership in the use of smart cards throughout the 1980s. Chip miniaturization allowed the smart card to be slimmed down to the point where it looks like a normal credit card. By the end of 1987, approximately 3.6 million smart cards were carried in French wallets.

These so-called fourth-generation cards (third-generation being cards with read-write magnetic tracks) offered some advantages to the issuers: they were more secure than earlier cards, and they could be used for off-line debits. The security advantage stemmed from the storage of the PIN in the embedded chip. When placed in a relatively inexpensive off-line authorization terminal, the customer entered his or her PIN, which was then checked for accuracy by the chip. Thus, lost or stolen cards could not be easily used by thieves. Storage of a PIN on a magnetic stripe was not nearly as secure because the magnetic stripe could be easily read and altered.

The second advantage of smart cards for issuers was how easily they could be used in off-line debits: the card could be "charged up" with a deposit and would reduce its balance with each payment. This feature is particularly important for debit use involving interchanges between banks, cities, or countries. The cost of facilitating an electronic debit in Norway for a French user would involve a much higher communications expenditure if done in real time than if done in a distributed mode through the smart card and settled in much cheaper batch mode. The greater number of intercountry transfers may help to explain why the smart card and other off-line EFT technologies have been more popular in Europe than in the United States.

The major obstacle to smart cards in the United States has been the much higher cost here of producing them—estimated to be four times the cost of a standard credit card with a magnetic stripe. The cost differential does not diminish significantly even when they are produced in bulk. The cards also lack consumer appeal. Most U.S. consumers consider the smart card inferior to a checkbook because it does not allow them to see the remaining balance unless it is read through a special terminal.

U.S. resistance to the smart card has prompted the development of the fifth-generation SuperSmart card by Toshiba for Visa. It looks something like a solar-powered calculator with a small display screen and keys, as well as an internal battery. Balances can be read at any time by the consumer who follows the self-contained instructions. Field tests of how easily consumers learned to use this card were begun in Japan in 1988 at the Hankyu department store in the Yurakucho district of Tokyo, but it is too early to say how successful this latest smart card will be.

Although its primary function has always been and continues to be a simple one—to identify the cardholder—the credit card has evolved into a tremendously sophisticated instrument in an increasingly complex world. Much of the focus of credit card design has been on securing it from fraud. With the growth of EFT systems, however, the card is being engineered to perform ever more complex tasks. Few people realize the amount of thought and technological invention that has gone into these palm-sized rectangles we so offhandedly refer to as "plastic." However, as we have seen with the development of OCR and smart cards, the card and its technology will play a pivotal role in the future not only of the credit card industry but also of EFT systems.

CONCLUSION

WHEN ALFRED BLOOMINGDALE AND HIS partners Frank McNamara and Ralph Snyder started Diners Club in 1949, they could not have realized that their shoestring operation would trigger the development of a multibillion-dollar global industry. In the short span of forty years, the credit card has changed forever the way most consumers and merchants conduct business. The nearly four billion credit, debit, and check guarantee cards in circulation worldwide have become an integral part of our daily lives. Consumers seem to have taken the television commercial to heart: very few ever leave home without one.

The figures in the United States alone are impressive. By 1984, 71 percent of all families possessed a credit card. The most pronounced expansion has been achieved in the bank card industry: from 1970 to 1986, the number of families carrying a bank credit card increased from 16 to 55 percent. Sixty-two percent owned a retail card, and 34 percent owned a gas card. The most popular card by far was Visa, which was carried by 45.3 percent of all Americans between the ages of seventeen and sixty-five. It was followed by Sears (38.4 percent) and MasterCard (30.1 percent). The leading gas cards were Amoco, with 13.9 percent, and Shell, with 9.5 percent. American Express cards are held by 12.5 percent of the population, and 9.5 percent own a Discover card.

American Express continues to lead in charge volume by a considerable margin, with $74.3 billion. It is far ahead of its closest competitor, Citibank, which has $19.5 billion, and Sears, with $13.4 billion. Citibank leads in outstanding debt ($15 billion), followed closely by American Express and Sears.

To support the increase in consumer credit and to differentiate their products from those of their competitors, merchants have poured money into advertising budgets, enabling them to market more goods

153

more often and more effectively than ever before. Stores stay open later, and new, more convenient shopping centers and malls have been built to further increase consumer spending. Debt maturities on major items such as automobiles have grown from three to four to five years, and down payments have decreased as lenders and automakers compete for the consumer's business.

New forms of credit were created over the years to make borrowing more and more convenient. Credit instruments such as overdraft provisions, on-demand deposits, signature loans, and telephone auto loans greatly reduced the time and effort involved in obtaining credit. But the most significant new vehicle for consumer credit, and the one best suited to the postwar economic climate, was the credit card.

Ironically, even as consumer debt grew exponentially, surveys continued to indicate that most Americans still disapproved of it. However, this attitude has not stopped them from using it. Unlike Europeans and consumers in other countries, Americans have made considerable use of credit for most of the country's history. Despite contrary responses to surveys, American consumers' increasing reliance upon consumer credit supports the fact that they simply do not share the European bias against consumer credit.

The credit card industry has been a peculiarly American development. The credit card has evolved to meet the needs of our mobile, affluent society. Credit has always been available from local merchants, but as mobile customers began dealing with merchants over a larger geographic area, the personal trust that had existed between the merchant and his regular customers had to be replaced with the trust of a well-known third-party guarantor. The increased demand for both goods and credit brought on by greater affluence created an environment in which the credit card could flourish.

For the credit card companies, achieving this tremendous growth was neither simple nor always profitable. In fact, the bank cards, which now control most of the marketplace, either lost money or were only marginally profitable for most of the 1960s and 1970s. Only in the 1980s did they produce significant profits—which are already dwindling under the stress of increased competition.

Why have the credit card companies persevered year after year despite poor performance? For retailers and oil companies, the answer is obvious. They viewed their credit card operations as marketing tools rather than profit centers and so were willing to absorb losses to gain or retain market share. For T&E cards, as we have seen, low profitability was not a problem; they have been profitable concerns for most of their existence.

This leaves the bank card companies, for whom there appear to have been several reasons to persevere. Many believed that credit cards would eventually prove profitable, that if they could hold down costs and continue to increase revenues, eventually their operations would move from the red into the black. Perhaps the most important reason, particularly in the early days of the industry, was the banks' perception of a strong cross-selling potential in the cards. Credit cards in the beginning were closely identified with individual banks. If a bank did not offer a card, the customer was likely to move on to a rival bank, which could conceivably attract all of the customer's accounts. This fear is indicative of the imitative, almost lemminglike nature of the banking industry, which has always been quick to follow a trend, however unpromising, rather than be left behind.

For a few farsighted individuals—such as John Reed of Citibank and John Fisher of Bank One in Ohio—who were more knowledgeable about the technological implications of the credit card, the decision to remain in the field can be traced to a desire to get in on the ground floor of an industry that they believed would one day replace the credit card—EFT systems.

In November 1970, Dale Reistad of Payment Systems, Inc. told a bank card conference that the banking industry is "either taking a bath in developing a credit card system or is paying a small fee for entering the era of electronic funds transfer." Reistad, now head of the EFT Association, predicted the development of POS terminals that would replace credit card embossers; he also predicted that "credit card authorization will have a zero limit and some retailers will move to direct billing from terminal base transactions."

How close are we to Reistad's vision of the future? Still a long way off, it would seem. Although various EFT systems have become a part of our everyday lives, we have far to go in creating a world of totally paperless banking. Furthermore, the likelihood that EFT systems will replace credit cards appears remote. Aside from its convenience, many people have become dependent on the credit function of the credit card. Even if they pay off their balance each month, they have thirty days of extra money, money they can use to tide them over until they receive their weekly, biweekly, or monthly paycheck. Customers have resisted POS systems because their accounts would immediately be debited for money they either would rather keep for a few weeks or will not have until the next paycheck.

As the credit card industry moves toward the next century, it appears likely that it will continue to thrive and fill an important role in our society. While increased competition will probably prevent companies from reaping profits similar to those of the boom years of the 1980s, it is doubtful that the industry will return to making only the marginal profits of the 1970s. Technology, as it always has, will continue to play a significant role as the industry evolves to meet the needs of the marketplace.

CHRONOLOGY

1890	Traveler's check is invented by Marcellus F. Barry of American Express.
1910	Arthur J. Morris's bank makes first consumer loans; "Morris-plan" banks begin to proliferate.
1914	Retailers issue credit cards.
1928	First National City Bank of New York opens first personal loan department. Department stores begin distributing charga-plates to customers.
1931	Century Airlines issues coupon books.
1936	American Airlines forms UATP and invites other airlines to join plan.
late 1930s	Wanamaker's begins practice of revolving credit.
1939	Air Traffic Conference assumes control of UATP. Standard Oil of Indiana begins first major credit card marketing campaign, distributing 250,000 new cards.
1947	Flatbush National Bank, under John C. Biggins, issues local universal Charge-It card. William B. Gorman introduces rotating charge accounts to Gimbel Bros., as he had done at L. Bamberger & Company earlier.
1948	Major New York department stores form cooperative charga-plate operation.
1949	Diners Club is formed.
early 1950s	British Hotel and Restaurant Association forms BHR credit card. Bank cards proliferate; no annual fees are charged, but merchants are charged a discount.

1952	Standard Oil of California introduces Chevromatic charga-plates.
1955	More than 100 types of bank card are now extant.
1956	J. L. Hudson's of Detroit adds thirty-day interest-free period. Diners Club begins marketing insurance to cardholders.
1957	Oil companies refuse to honor universal third-party cards but agree to honor other gas cards.
1958	BankAmericard launches its credit card operation. Carte Blanche is founded. American Express enters universal credit card field. American Express takes over American Hotel Association's Universal Travel Card. Chase Manhattan launches CMCP.
1958–1959	Banks begin to charge interest on unpaid balances.
1962	Chase sells CMCP to Uni-Serve, which renames it Uni-Card.
1964	Airlines begin accepting T&E cards.
1965	BHR of Great Britain and Rikskort of Sweden join to form EuroCard International. Carte Blanche is sold to FNCB Services Corporation.
1966	Bank of America announces plan to license BankAmericard across the United States. Interbank Card Association is formed to compete with BankAmericard.
1967	Docutel is formed by Recognition Equipment, Inc.
1969	Interbank buys "Master Charge" name from Western States Bank Card Association. Chase acquires Uni-Card. NRMA begins a test: merchants pool credit operations while retaining individual identities. First Docutel cash dispenser is installed.
late 1960s	Bank card companies initiate mass mailings of unsolicited credit cards.
1970	FTC temporarily bans mailings of unsolicited cards. Permanent ban signed by President Nixon. TWA introduces Get-Away card, which can be used much like a T&E card. Bank of America spins off BankAmericard, forming NBI. Manufacturers Hanover Trust begins using a post-mailer and dual dating to deter mail theft of cards.

1971   GECC organizes credit card operation for NRMA. Atlantic Richfield turns over credit operations to National Data Corporation of Atlanta. Federal Reserve clarifies annual fee controversy by ruling it to be separate from finance charges. Worthen Bank and Trust, an NBI member, gains membership in Interbank; NBI passes amendment bylaw prohibiting dual card operations. First reported case of counterfeit credit cards, in Los Angeles.

1972   Court decides in favor of Worthen Bank and Trust, clearing the way for duality. NBI purchases Uni-Card from Chase. Carte Blanche issues its gold card. Fair Credit Billing Act is passed, giving Federal Reserve Board power to regulate billing practices.

1973   UATP issues silver card, in response to T&E competition. NBI begins operation of BASE I, national credit authorization system designed by IBM. Marquette Bank of Minnesota becomes first to charge an annual fee for its credit card. Atlantic Richfield and Docutel introduce automatic gas-dispensing machines. NBI amends bylaws to allow mutual savings banks to become members. Oil embargo swells numbers of gas cardholders. Wells Fargo initiates its Gold Account program.

1974   BankAmericard forms Ibanco to administer accounts in Europe. American Express allows merchants to offer cash discounts to customers. Federal Privacy Act is passed. First six OCR systems able to read UPC codes are installed.

1975   Bank of America switches to calculating finance charge on average daily balance, which becomes industry norm. Wells Fargo signs with First Data Resources to begin Well Service, a private-label credit card program for retailers. American Express issues its gold card. Citibank purchases Carte Blanche. Forming an agreement with Isra-Card, Interbank is first to penetrate Israeli market. Current version of Fair Credit Billing Act is passed. Equal Credit Opportunity Act is passed. U.S. Privacy Protection Study Commission begins two-year investigation of credit industry. First National Bank of Atlanta begins Honest Face check verification program.

1976   NBI changes "BankAmericard" to "Visa". NBI gives up its opposition to duality. Citibank announces 50-cent monthly charge on all paid-up accounts. Wanamaker's and other Philadelphia retailers temporarily agree to accept universal cards to take advantage of Bicentennial tourist trade. American Express installs traveler's check dispensers in airports. Visa issues Entree, its first debit card. Swiss banks appoint Electrowatt of Zurich to develop a comprehensive ATM system. Regulation Q begins phase out, eliminating ceilings on interest that banks can pay on deposits.

1977   State Savings and Loan of Stockton, California, becomes first thrift institution to be granted proprietary license for a bank card. GECC purchases Woolworth credit operation. Final version of Equal Credit Opportunity Act is passed. American Express begins Centurion Service.

1978   Citibank drops 50-cent charge on paid-up accounts, noting that it had made its credit operation profitable while in effect. Visa issues first custom card—with Pay-n-Save in Seattle—carrying two logos. Financial Institutions Regulatory and Interest Rate Control Act, prohibiting tracking of credit card purchases, is passed. Inter Conto of Sweden becomes first nonbank issuer of Visa card in Europe. Electronic Funds Transfer Act is passed. Citibank discontinues its check guarantee plan.

1979   Visa and J. C. Penney reach accord. Gas crisis prompts oil companies to again stop honoring third-party cards. Chase drops its Master Charge operation.

1980   Interbank changes "Master Charge" to "MasterCard." Citibank purchases Diners Club. CAB turns down lawsuit by credit card issuers challenging UATP silver card as a restriction on competition. Bank One of Columbus, Ohio, begins its Channel 2000 home-banking experiment. President Jimmy Carter announces establishment of credit controls; banks respond by imposing annual credit card fees.

1981   Texaco charges 3 percent fee on credit card transactions to dealers, who respond by offering discounts for cash purchases. MasterCard launches its gold card.

1982   Key Federal Savings and Loan (Maryland) launches its secured credit card operation. Atlantic Richfield drops its card operations; dealers are permitted to accept other cards if they wish to pay the merchant's discount. Olivetti acquires Docutel. Visa launches its Premier card (later changed to Visa Gold).

1984   Bank card use peaks, with 71 percent of all Americans between seventeen and sixty-five carrying a card.

1985   First affinity cards are launched by Visa and MasterCard.

1986   Sears launches Discover card. Bank One of Columbus, Ohio, introduces first securities backed by credit card receivables by issuing $50 million in CARDs. Tax Reform Act of 1986 begins phaseout of credit card interest deduction.

1987   American Express launches Optima card.

1988   Fifth-generation SuperSmart card is introduced at Hankyu department store in Tokyo. First Data Resources acquires Eastern States Bank Card Association. GECC acquires Montgomery Ward credit card portfolio. Fair Credit and Charge Card Disclosure Act is passed.

1989   Visa introduces VisaPhone telephone charge service.

BIBLIOGRAPHIC ESSAY

THE LITERATURE ON CREDIT CARDS IS EX-
tensive and varied, in both purpose and quality. There are books aimed at
consumers, ranging from Howard Strong, *Credit Card Secrets You Will
Surely Profit From* to Melvin Pierre, Sr., *How to Get a Visa Or MasterCard . . . Even Though You May Have Previously Been Turned Down.*
Numerous magazine and newspaper articles also deal with the wise use of
credit cards.

Many articles and a few books have been aimed at those in the credit
card and related industries. A recent compact-disk search using the phrase
"credit card" yielded more than a thousand articles in business publications
in the past half-dozen years alone.

Scholarly work has also been done on the subject. Some of it, such as
my own book *Credit Card Use in the United States,* focuses on card usage
among consumers. But most scholarly work has focused on the impact of
credit cards and electronic funds transfer on the monetary system, especially on the demand for money.

Since the credit card industry employs tens of thousands of people,
textbooks have been written to train new entrants. The first such book,
written in 1976 for the American Bankers Association by Neil Murphy and
myself, was entitled *Bank Cards.* Of more recent vintage is Duane
Krummes's *Banking and the Plastic Card* (1987).

However, until now there have been few attempts to write a comprehensive history of credit cards. In fact, most of the "history" of credit cards
that is occasionally cited in newspaper and magazine articles appears to
come from two articles: Frederick M. Struble's "Bank Credit Cards and
Check Credit Plans in the Nation and the District" (1969), and Irwin Ross's
"The Credit Card's Painful Coming-of-Age" (1971). By far the best history
to date was written by Gerd J. Weisensee, whose small monograph has been
published only in German.

The analysis contained in this book is based upon five distinct sources

162

of information. For the period preceding the beginning of the modern credit card industry with the formation of Diners Club in 1949, most of the historical material comes from books on business and economic history, including some company histories. The very early history of credit is covered in Paul Einzig's book *Primitive Money* (1949), in George Goodspeed's classic textbook, *A History of the Ancient World* (1904), and in Charles O. Hardy's *Consumer Credit and Its Uses* (1938).

Somewhat more recently, Herbert Heaton's *Economic History of Europe* (1948) describes the use of consumer credit from the Middle Ages into the industrial era. Rolf Nugent's *Consumer Credit and Economic Stability* (1939) gives good coverage to the early use of credit in the United States.

The discussion of the early years of Diners Club is based upon an interview with Alfred Bloomingdale, one of the founders of Diners Club, shortly before his death, supplemented with newspaper and magazine coverage of the period. My own experience as an early (and perhaps the only) scholar in the field for twenty years put me in direct contact with many of the pioneers of the credit card industry in the United States and abroad. These contacts have helped fill in many of the gaps.

The role of today's Citibank as a pioneer in the field of consumer credit and as a major player in the modern history of credit cards is detailed in *Citibank, 1812–1970* by Harold Cleveland and Thomas Huertas. The on-again–off-again position of Chase Manhattan Bank as a credit card innovator is covered in John David Wilson's *The Chase: The Chase Manhattan Bank, N.A., 1945–1985*.

Another useful piece documenting the early years of credit card growth is Robert Johnson's article, "Nation-Spanning Credit Cards." The Weisensee monograph cited above, as well as my own 1972 book and the articles by Struble and Ross, give the clearest outline of the period.

The third, and most important, source of historical information used in this book is the biweekly *Nilson Report*, which has been published since 1970, a period spanning half of the existence of the modern credit card. Spencer Nilson, who worked for Diners Club during its early years, has given extensive, ongoing coverage to the industry in an unparalleled manner. As mentioned in the preface, it was at his request and with his newsletter that the research for this book was undertaken. Unless otherwise specified in the text, statistical figures are derived from twice-monthly issues of the *Nilson Report*.

Materials on electronic funds transfer are far easier to find than those relating to credit cards, perhaps because the subject is perceived to be sexier. A number of books have been written on the subject, including Robert Hendrickson's *The Cashless Society*, Patrick Kirkman's *Electronic Funds Transfer Systems: The Revolution in Cashless Banking and Payments Methods*, which describes EFT in Great Britain, *Electronic Banking* by Alan

Lipis, et al., and J. R. S. Revell's *Banking and Electronic Fund Transfers*, which covers EFT in Europe.

Finally, I have used hundreds of newspaper and magazine articles and government reports to supplement and document the sources given above. The selected bibliography lists books and theses that have dealt with credit cards and a few important articles and reports that may be helpful to future scholars in the field.

SELECTED
BIBLIOGRAPHY

Aboucher, Roger J. "Bank Charge Cards in the 1970s." *Banking,* October 1969.

————, and Nicholas E. Magnis. "Bank Credit Cards—Implications for the Future." *Bankers Monthly,* January 1967.

Adams, Kenneth M. *The Bank Card: Yesterday, Today, and Tomorrow.* Washington, D.C.: American Bankers Association, Bank Card Division, September 1974.

Alm, Raymond H. *Charge Account Banking.* Thesis, Rutgers University, 1962.

American Bankers Association. *Bank Card Fact Book.* Washington, D.C.: ABA, 1979.

————, *Credit Card Survey.* (ABA National Automation Conference). Washington, D.C.: ABA, 1967.

Bender, Mark G. *Electronic Funds Transfer Systems: Elements and Inputs.* Port Washington, N.Y.: Kennikat Press, 1975.

Bequai, August. *The Cashless Society: EFT at the Crossroads.* New York: John Wiley & Sons, 1981.

Bosworth, William Cyrus. *Unused Credit and the Demand for Money.* Ph.D. thesis, University of Connecticut, 1985.

Boult, Raymond. "France Puts Its Money on the Smart Cards." *Systems International* (U.K.), March 1988.

Bray, S. E. "Credit Card Fraud Can Be Controlled If Precautions Are Observed." *Mid-Continent Banker,* April 1970.

Brennan, Edward J. "The Changing Face of Charge Account Banking." *Credit World,* September 1968.

Canner, Glenn B. "Changes in Consumer Holding and Use of Credit Cards, 1970–86." *Journal of Retail Banking,* Spring 1988.

Chin, Felix. *Electronic Funds Transfers: A Selected Bibliography.* Monticello, Ill.: Council of Planning Librarians, 1978.

Cleveland, Harold van B., and Thomas F. Huertas. *Citibank, 1812–1970.* Cambridge, Mass.: Harvard University Press, 1985.

Cloos, George W., and Edward W. Birgells. "Bank Credit Cards." *Business Conditions* (Federal Reserve Bank of Chicago), July 1972.

Cocheo, Steve. "Bank Cards at the Crossroads." *ABA Banking Journal,* September 1987.

Cole, Robert H. *Consumer and Commercial Credit Management.* Homewood, Ill.: Richard D. Irwin, 1976.

Colton, Kent, and Kenneth L. Kraemer, eds. *Computers and Banking: Electronic Funds Transfer Systems and Public Policy.* New York: Plenum Press, 1980.

Einzig, Paul. *Primitive Money.* London: Erie and Spottiswoode, 1949.

Federal Reserve Bank of Atlanta. *Payments in the Financial Services Industry in the 1980s.* Westport, Conn.: Quorum Books, 1984.

Federal Reserve System, Board of Governors. *1977 Consumer Credit Survey.* Washington, D.C.: Board of Governors of the Federal Reserve System, 1978.

Franklin, T. C. "The Significance of Interchange for Bank Credit Plans." *Burroughs Clearing House,* August 1968.

Freeman, Laurie, and Kate Fitzgerald. "Sears May Hold Winning Card—Pros pects Brighten for Discover." *Advertising Age,* 18 January 1988.

Giblin, Thomas J. "Buying Accounts Receivables in Bank Card Plans." *Credit World,* February 1969.

Gibson, Donald M. *A Study of the Strategic and Operational Significance of the Credit Card for Commercial Banks.* Boston: Harvard University, Graduate School of Business Administration, 1967.

Goodspeed, George Stephen. *A History of the Ancient World.* New York: Scribner's, 1904.

Graham, Judith. "Affinity Card Clutter." *Advertising Age,* 14 November 1988.

Hansell, Saul. "Card Wars." *Institutional Investor,* May 1988.

Hardy, Charles O., et al. *Consumer Credit and Its Uses.* New York: Prentice-Hall, 1938.

Heaton, Herbert. *Economic History of Europe.* New York: Harper and Brothers, 1948.

Hendrickson, Robert A. *The Cashless Society.* New York: Dodd, Mead, 1972.

Hull, Everette D., and Leslie Annand. "Time to Jump on the Securitization Bankwagon?" *ABA Banking Journal,* October 1987.

Johnson, Robert. "Nation-Spanning Credit Cards." *Monthly Review* (Federal Reserve Bank of San Francisco), March 1972.

Kessler, Richard T. *Marketing Implications for Bank Consumer Revolving Credit.* Master's thesis, New York University, 1966.

Kirkman, Patrick. *Electronic Funds Transfer Systems: The Revolution in Cashless Banking and Payment Methods.* Oxford, England: Basil Blackwell, 1987.

Krumme, Duane. *Banking and the Plastic Card.* Washington, D.C.: American Bankers Association, 1987.

Kuroda, Iwao. "Electronic Systems Developments in Retail Banking in Japan." *World of Banking,* July/August 1987.

Larkin, Kenneth V. "Launching a National Credit Card." *Pacific Banker and Business,* October 1966.

Levy, Robert. "Clash of the Credit Cards." *Dun's Review,* June 1978.

Lipis, Allan H., Thomas R. Marschall, and Jan H. Linker. *Electronic Banking.* New York: Wiley, 1985.

Mandell, Lewis. "Credit Cards and the Financing of Small Business," in Paul M. Horvitz and R. Richardson Pettit, eds., *Small Business Finance: Sources of Financing for Small Business.* Greenwich, Conn.: JAI Press, 1984.

————. *Economics from the Consumer's Perspective.* Palo Alto, Calif.: Science Research Associates, 1975.

————. "Consumer Knowledge and Opinions of Consumer Credit." *Journal of Consumer Credit Management,* Fall 1973.

————. *Credit Card Use in the United States.* Ann Arbor, Mich.: Institute for Social Research, 1972.

————, and Neil B. Murphy. *Bank Cards.* Washington, D.C.: American Institute of Banking of the American Bankers Association, 1976.

————, and Neil B. Murphy. "Personal Service in Banking". Storrs, Conn.: Center for Research and Development in Financial Services, December, 1987.

Martin, Claude R. *An Introduction to Electronic Funds Transfer Systems.* New York: American Management Association, 1978.

Miller, Frederic A. "How AMEX Is Revamping Its Big, Beautiful Money Machine." *Business Week,* 13 June 1988.

Modi, Meena. "POS Microcosm." *ABA Banking Journal,* October 1987.

Morris, David Mark. *Selling and Securitizing Commercial Bank Assets.* Thesis, Stonier Graduate School of Banking, 1987.

Murphy, Neil B., and Lewis Mandell. *NOW Accounts.* Park Ridge, Ill.: Bank Administration Institute, 1980.

Nilson Report. 1972 to present. Bimonthly newsletter written and published by Spensor Nilson, Santa Monica, Calif.

Niman, Neil Bruce. *The Economics of an Electronic System of Exchange.* Ph.D. thesis, University of Texas at Austin, 1985.

Nugent, Rolf. *Consumer Credit and Economic Stability.* New York: Russell Sage Foundation, 1939.

Patterson, Harlan R. *A Study of Charge Account Banking and Its Financial Performance.* Ph.D. thesis, Michigan State University, 1963.

Payment Systems Research Program. *Bank Credit Cards: Payment vs. Credit Usage.* New York: Payment Systems, Inc., 1979.

Pierre, Melvin, Sr. *How to Get a Visa or MasterCard . . . Even Though You May Have Previously Been Turned Down.* RPM Finanical Consulting, 1986.

Pullen, Robert W. "Bank Credit Card and Related Plans." *New England Business Review* (Federal Reserve Bank of Boston), December 1966.

Reistad, Dale L. "Credit Cards—Stepping Stones to the Checkless Society." *Computers and Automation*, January 1967.

Revell, J. R. S. *Banking and Electronic Fund Transfers.* Paris: Organization for Economic Development and Cooperation, 1983.

Ross, Irwin. "The Credit Card's Painful Coming-of-Age." *Fortune*, October 1971.

Russell, Thomas. *The Economics of Bank Credit Cards.* New York: Praeger, 1975.

Seiders, David. "Credit Cards and Check-Credit Plans at Commercial Banks." *Federal Reserve Bulletin*, September 1973.

Shay, Robert, and William C. Dunkelberg. *Retail Store Credit Card Use in New York.* New York: Columbia University, 1975.

Shogase, Hiro. "The Very Smart Card: A Plastic Pocket Book." *IEEE Spectrum*, October 1988.

Sloan, Irving J. *Law and Legislation of Credit Card Use and Misuse.* New York: Oceana Publications, 1987.

Smith, James F. "The Equal Credit Opportunity Act of 1974: A Cost/Benefit Analysis." *Journal of Finance* 32 (2 November 1977): 609–22.

Strong, Howard. *Credit Card Secrets You Will Surely Profit From.* Boswell Corp., 1989.

Struble, Frederick. "Bank Credit Cards and Check Credit Plans in the Nation and the District." *Monthly Review* (10th Federal Reserve District), July–August 1969.

Tadlock, Bill Carthan. *A Model to Predict Bank Credit Card Usage Patterns.* Ph.D. thesis, Mississippi State University, 1980.

Touche, Ross, Bailey, and Smart. "Economic Characteristics of Department Store Credit." A report for the National Retail Merchants Association, 1967.

U.S. Congress, Conference Committees, *Equal Credit Opportunity Act: Conference Report to Accompany H.R. 6516.* Washington, D.C.: U.S. Government Printing Office, 1976.

U.S. Congress, House Committee on Banking, Finance, and Urban Affairs,

Fair Credit and Charge Card Disclosure Act of 1987. Washington, D.C.: U.S. Government Printing Office, 1987.

————. *Electronic Fund Transfer Act: Report Together with Additional and Dissenting Views to Accompany H.R. 13007.* Washington, D.C.: U.S. Government Printing Office, 1978.

————, Subcommittee on Consumer Affairs and Coinage. *To Amend the Equal Credit Opportunity Act: Hearing,* 99th Cong. 2d sess. 12 August 1986.

U.S. Department of Commerce. *Retail Credit Survey,* January–June 1931, series 53. Washington, D.C.: U.S. Government Printing Office, 1932.

"Universal Credit Card." *National Petroleum News,* 19 November 1952.

Watro, Paul R. "The Bank Credit-Card Boom: Some Explanations and Consequences." *Economic Commentary* (Federal Reserve Bank of Cleveland), March 1988.

Weisensee, Gerd J. *Die Kreditkarte—ein Amerikanisches Phanomen.* Bern, Switzerland: Paul Haupt, 1970.

Wilson, John David. *The Chase: The Chase Manhattan Bank, N.A., 1945–1985.* Boston: Harvard Business School Press, 1986.

Wittfeld, Paul. "Automation and Technology Report: Smart Cards Today and in the Future." *Magazine of Bank Administration,* August 1986.

Zimmer, Linda Fenner. "ATMs: An Industry Status Report/ATM Directory." *Bank Administration,* May 1987.

INDEX

THE AUTHOR

LEWIS MANDELL IS PROFESSOR OF FINANCE at the University of Connecticut's School of Business Administration. His involvement in the credit card industry began in the late 1960s when he directed the Surveys of Consumer Finances at the University of Michigan's Survey Research Center. At the suggestion of colleague George Katona, he added questions concerning credit card use to the annual surveys. An analysis of these questions resulted in his *Credit Card Use in the United States* (1972), the first scholarly book examining this phenomenon. His second book, *Bank Cards* (1976), coauthored with Neil B. Murphy, is a textbook for aspiring credit card bankers.

Mandell has been long involved with electronic funds transfer, serving as a speaker, researcher, and writer on the subject as well as a consultant to many large banks and equipment manufacturers. As director of research for the U.S. comptroller of the currency he represented his office on the Electronic Funds Transfer Commission.